PILGRIM PRAYERS FOR
PEOPLE LIVING WITH CANCER

PILGRIM PRAYERS FOR
People Living with Cancer

Susan M. Northey

The Pilgrim Press

Cleveland

Dedication
*I dedicate this book to all the courageous individuals that were
inspired to share their personal stories with me. Thank you for this
profound, heartfelt gift.*

The Pilgrim Press, 700 Prospect Avenue East, Cleveland, Ohio 44115-1100
thepilgrimpress.com

© 2004 by Susan M. Northey

Biblical quotations are from the *New Revised Standard Version Bible,* © copyright 1989 by the
Division of Christian Education of the National Council of the Churches of Christ in the
U.S.A., and are used by permission.

08   07   06   05   04   5 4 3 2 1

Library of Congress Cataloging-in-Publication Data

Northey, Susan M., 1958–
    Pilgrim prayers for people living with cancer / Susan M. Northey.
        p.   cm.
    ISBN 0-8298-1586-4 (pbk. : alk. paper)
    1. Cancer—Patients—Prayer-books and devotions—English.   I. Title.

BV4910.33.N67 2004
242'.4—dc22   2004053545

All last names were changed within this book to respect the privacy of those interviewed.

Contents

Acknowledgments

THERE ARE MANY TO THANK for the accomplishment of this book.

My husband, John, and my children, Bryan, Matthew, and Katelyn for being extremely supportive as I spent countless hours interviewing people and writing and editing this book.

My parents, Don and Mary, who taught me that I could accomplish whatever I wanted, as long as I put my heart and soul into it.

The Pilgrim Press and my editor, Kim Sadler, who believed in me–a first-time author–and allowed me to share these inspirational stories with so many people who are in need.

Carolyn Bellin, Director of Public Relations for Froedtert Hospital, for supporting my efforts and introducing me to numerous cancer patients, survivors, and caregivers.

And, most of all, the Lord above, who first allowed me to become a cancer survivor and then provided me with the inspiration and means to write this book.

ONE

My Calling

M Y HUSBAND, MY MOTHER, AND I were on the way to the hospital with heavy hearts and heightened anxiety. Today would be the day. The day that would either liberate us from our nagging fears or the day that would symbolize the beginning of a challenging new chapter in our lives. Today I was scheduled for a surgical biopsy to determine if the growth the doctors had discovered in my chest was malignant or benign. My husband and mother were allowed to stay with me until the anesthesiologist came into the room to prep me for surgery. I so appreciated them being there. They kept me distracted, talking about anything and everything except the situation at hand. They held my hand and reassured me without saying a word. The only sign of my mother's fear was her slightly trembling lower lip.

And then, I was by myself. I felt alone, cold, and terribly frightened. I tried to mentally prepare myself for the bad biopsy results I strongly suspected I would have within the hour. I prayed fervently and desperately, "Please, Lord, don't let it be cancer. Please, Lord, don't let it be cancer." Over and over again, I prayed.

All of a sudden, an amazing sense of tranquility flooded my senses. My body stopped trembling and I felt as if I were ensconced in a blanket of comforting warmth. Suddenly my mind was filled with a message. "You have Hodgkin's. But don't worry—you will live." There was no disputing the meaning of this message or where it came from. I instantly knew, with 100% certainty, that I had Hodgkin's *and* that I would live.

Shortly thereafter, the anesthesiologist wheeled me into the operating room. While I waited for the anesthetic to take effect, the nurse removed a blanket from an oven and covered me. It seemed like such an insignificant gesture, but it was so comforting. The next thing I knew, I was back in the recovery room and the surgeon was sadly informing me that I had lymphoma. I cried three tears–one, two, three–and stopped, for I knew with all my heart that my time on this earth was far from over. Two days later, New Year's Eve, my doctor called and confirmed that I had Hodgkin's lymphoma. Happy New Year!

Being a perpetual optimist, I've always believed that "everything in life happens for a reason." So I truly never asked *why* I had been diagnosed with this terrible disease. Surprisingly, I never felt anger nor did I wage a war with God. I just found myself searching for that *one* key insight that would clearly help me devise an action plan. I surmised that maybe I had been inflicted with cancer because I was strong and would be able to help others who needed assistance through this same journey at some point in their lives.

It wasn't until I was about a month into my diagnosis that I realized that this wasn't the case at all. I was coming out of my bedroom one morning when my mind filled with yet another message, "That's *not* why you got it." As you can well imagine, this stopped me dead in my tracks. Of course, I asked, "Well then, why *did* I get it?" The answer I received was, "So you can teach people that faith heals." Now I had to chuckle a bit. I liked my idea better . . . this was a lot tougher challenge as far as I was concerned. As a child growing up, my family was fairly private about their faith. Now all of a sudden I was faced with a calling that went well beyond my comfort level.

I remembered talking to a friend of mine, Julie, about her decision to go to seminary. She told me that there is no denying your calling, no matter how hard you try. If it is meant to be, it will be. So, I gave in . . . slowly at first. I began talking to my faithful friends about my deepest thoughts. Then I branched out to my family, explaining how my prayers *were* working; they were making a real difference in my life.

Then one day, on the way home from work, something astonishing happened. I began writing a sermon in my head. The words flowed effort-lessly and miraculously, and I realized that the Spirit had moved me. This was my calling. I needed to help others understand that belief in God is powerful and that their faith can help them navigate the stormy and turbulent times in life.

This series of experiences triggered a spiritual, mental, emotional, and physical journey unlike any I had ever taken before. I began a difficult, but inspiring, time of self-discovery. I responded to God's call in the ways I knew best. I gave a sermon at church, wrote one book and then another, helped others going through their cancer journeys, taught healing through journaling classes, spoke at numerous cancer-related events, and accepted a position on the Board of Directors for the Froedtert Hospital Foundation.

But something continued to nag at me. I wondered to myself, "If faith heals, then why do *so many* faithful people die?" It was an inconsistency that I just couldn't seem to reconcile.

It wasn't until four years later that I finally obtained clarification on my calling. I was walking through a labyrinth with the confirmation class from my church, meditating over my life and its purpose. As I walked, I suddenly felt a shudder go through my body and I was filled with the answer. I then came to understand that I had interpreted "faith heals" in the most literal of senses–healing the physical body. This theory hadn't worked for me, because faith doesn't always heal the body. We are, after all, merely mortals. But faith can heal in *so many* other ways–spiritually, mentally, emotionally. Faith can prepare us for death from this earthly place and can promise us eternal life.

I wondered, "Why didn't I have the vision to see this before?" It seemed so very simple. But then I realized that I would not have been able to cope with the possibility that I was so very vulnerable the year I had cancer. The Lord had waited until I was ready to comprehend the magnitude of His message.

It is important to remember that faith has the capacity to heal us in both spirit and mind. If the cancer consumes our body, despite our devout faith, it does not mean that we have lost in the end. Rather, just the converse is true. If we believe in Him, we have won.

. . .

I was pushed hard, so that I was falling, but the Lord helped me. The Lord is my strength and my might; he has become my salvation. There are glad songs of victory in the tents of the righteous; the right hand of the Lord does valiantly; the right hand of the Lord is exalted. I shall not die, but I shall live, and recount the deeds of the Lord.

—Psalm 118:13–17

Here I am, God. You have called, and I have answered you. Please inspire me to help others understand the power of your goodness and the virtue of your wisdom. As you did with me, please open others' minds to the wisdom of the phrase, "Faith heals." Amen.

TWO

Jesus Loves Me

A NNETTE WAS FIVE YEARS OLD and fast approaching the end of her too-short life. She had been ill for as long as she could remember. She had something the doctors called Whelms tumor or cancer of the kidney. Annette didn't really understand what Whelms was, but she knew it wasn't good. It seemed to make all the adults so sad whenever they talked about it.

Annette tried not to think of it very often, but today she was particularly frightened. It wasn't the pain. She was used to that. In fact, she couldn't remember a time in her life when she didn't have some discomfort or pain. No, today Annette was having a hard time because she was afraid of dying. She really didn't know what happened after you died. She wondered to herself, "Is heaven a *real* place where I can live forever? Will I still be able to talk to my mommy and daddy when I'm there?" She just didn't know, and so Annette was afraid.

Even though Annette had been raised in a Christian household, she had rarely felt well enough to attend church or go to Sunday School with all the other children. So she didn't really have the answers to her questions. But then one day Grandpa Aberle came to visit Annette. Grandpa was an ordained minister and he thought it was time to teach Annette all about God and Jesus. Grandpa spent several hours with Annette one sunny afternoon. He taught her about Jesus' love and explained how Jesus welcomed little children into His kingdom. He read Scripture verses to Annette and explained what the verses meant in words that Annette could understand. Annette thought the stories he told her were really good ones and she enjoyed them a great deal. Later, Grandpa taught Annette the words to the song "Jesus Loves Me." Together, their voices rang throughout the house:

"Jesus loves me. This I know, for the Bible tells me so. Little ones to Him belong; they are weak, but He is strong. Yes, Jesus loves me. Yes, Jesus loves me. Yes, Jesus loves me. The Bible tells me so."

The hours Annette spent with Grandpa Aberle flew by. As each hour passed, so did Annette's fear. Until finally, when it was time for him to leave, Annette felt different. She felt calmer. While it had only been a few short hours, those hours had changed five-year-old Annette's life. She no longer feared death, for she had found comfort in the Lord. She welcomed the opportunity to join Jesus in His eternal kingdom, where she would live forever with no pain. And so on June 20, 1967, Annette passed from this world into God's kingdom, full of hope and joy, with a look of supreme peace on her face.

A few years after Annette's passing, her mother brought another beautiful girl into the world, named Judy. While Judy did not have the good fortune to ever get to know her older sister, her parents kept Annette's spirit alive in their household and in Judy's heart. So it was not too surprising that thirty-three years to the day of Annette's passing–June 20, 2000, —Judy gave birth to her own child, a beautiful baby girl she named Mary. It seemed so perfect. It was as if Mary was Annette's gift to the sister she had never known . . . one perfect little girl to symbolically replace the perfect little girl that had come before her.

. . .

At that time the disciples came to Jesus and asked, "Who is the greatest in the kingdom of heaven?" He called a child, whom he put among them, and said, "Truly I tell you, unless you change and become like children, you will never enter the kingdom of heaven. Whoever becomes humble like this child is the greatest in the kingdom of heaven. Whoever welcomes one such child in my name welcomes me."

—Matthew 18:1–5

God, it is sometimes difficult to understand why our children are taken from us. They are so young and innocent and so full of hope, love, and promise. We look upon them and are saddened that they had so little time to experience life. We wonder why you didn't take one of us instead, who had already lived a rich and full life. But, at the same time, we understand that your will must be done and that your kingdom also needs the exuberance and energy of our children. Thank you for helping us through these difficult times and for providing us with blessings that help to remind us of those that came before us. Amen.

THREE

A Modern Miracle

P ATRICIA WAS ON HER WAY TO HER oncologist's office to obtain the results of her recent CAT scan. Even though she had been having clean scans for the last two years, she always got nervous and on edge on the eve of her appointments. She found herself wondering, "What if the cancer is back? What will I do if I receive bad news? How can I possibly go through cancer *again*?" The questions churned through her mind.

Patti waited patiently in the examining room for the test results. When her oncologist entered the room, she knew in an instant that she wouldn't be hearing the news that she so longed to hear. His face had told her otherwise; it had concern written all over it. In a few short minutes, Patti heard the terrible words that she had prayed she would never hear again, "Your cancer is back." If that wasn't bad enough, there was more disturbing news. The doctor informed Patricia that the cancer had metastasized from her breast into one of her lungs. She listened with numb shock as he told her that the tumor was big, so big that they would not be able to remove it surgically. He went on to explain that unfortunately she could no longer receive radiation therapy or any of the chemotherapy drugs she had been given in the past because she had met her lifetime dosages of each in her previous two battles with breast cancer.

Patricia's mind raced as her doctor told her she desperately needed a stem cell transplant. Without it, he explained, her odds of survival were meager . . . only 1 to 2%. Even with the transplant, she had no more than a 15 to 20% chance of living.

As Patti reeled from the impact of the news, she steeled her resolve. She had approached her cancer with a positive and faithful attitude in the past and had emerged victorious. She had prayed fervently for re- covery, and God had answered her prayers each time. In her mind, He would just have to answer her prayers again because she was determined to live.

But as she put the wheels in motion to schedule her transplant, her path to recovery took another unexpected turn. Her insurance company denied the claim, explaining that the $150,000 stem cell transplant was considered "experimental" treatment. It fell outside the realm of normal insurance claims and, therefore, would not be approved. Patti desperately wrote letter after letter, asking for a policy change. She phoned in appeal after appeal, begging for compassion. She asked the personnel department of the company her husband worked for to call the insurance company to put pressure on them to pay. But it was all to no avail. The claim was rejected time and time again.

Patricia was stunned. She had endured *so much* over the last several years. Now she was being forced to deal with a reoccurrence of cancer, more emotional and physical pain, a stem cell transplant, and the pain of trying to figure out how she was going to pay for this surgery. She thought, "How can this all be happening? It's just not fair. How much can *one* person be expected to endure?" It was a nightmare, a real-life, never-ending nightmare.

Just when Patti thought that her odds of surviving all of this chaos were unlikely, miraculous things began to happen. The company she worked for held a fund-raiser in her honor, raising a substantial amount of money. Then, to her astonishment, an anonymous donor stepped forward with a $50,000 donation. She had the money she needed for her transplant.

Patricia endured the surgery and the weeks of isolation afterwards as her body's immune system struggled to repair itself. As she approached the time when treatment would begin, a new non-FDA-approved drug miraculously became available to Patti just in the nick of time. She began her treatment protocol, which involved several grueling months of chemotherapy. The bone pain that wracked her body was so excruciating that at times she found it difficult to walk from one office to the next, to climb the stairs to her bedroom in the evening, or just to live her life. She became best friends with Vicadin™, a strong painkiller, which mercifully allowed her to function. Through it all, Patti held her faith close at hand.

She continued to work whenever possible, inspiring her coworkers with her positive and faithful attitude.

At last her treatment protocol was complete. Patricia was scheduled for a CT so that her doctors could gauge just how effective the stem cell transplant and chemotherapy treatments had been. Once again, Patti found herself waiting with apprehension in her doctor's office for the results of her tests. But this time, he faced her with a look of unexpected pleasure, telling Patti that the tumor was now small enough to surgically remove.

Shortly thereafter, Patti underwent a successful lung surgery. For the third time she had survived the rigors of cancer. Through the grace of God, Patricia had been snatched out of the hands of death. The meager survival rate of 1 to 2% that she had first heard from her oncologist was now a thing of the past. She was alive thanks to the miracle that God had granted her.

. . .

O Lord my God, I cried to you for help, and you have healed me. . .
You have turned my mourning into dancing; you have taken off my
sackcloth and clothed me with joy, so that my soul may praise you
and not be silent. O Lord my God, I will give thanks to you forever.
—Psalm 30:2, 11–12

Dear God, at times, it feels as if we are overwhelmed with bad news. We question you, wondering why we have to deal with our heavy load. But it is through our struggle . . . to overcome that we come to know your true greatness. Thank you for carrying us through the challenging times in our lives, for putting us back on our feet at the end of our difficult journeys, and for granting miracles to remind us of your innate ability to heal. Amen.

FOUR

A Celebration of Life

❦

S HE WAS A TEACHER. It was the perfect career for Kris because she absolutely adored children. But as much as Kris loved her job, she would have given it all up in a heartbeat . . . to become a mother. Being a mom was all she had ever wanted out of life, all that she had ever hoped and prayed for.

Kris and Andy had been trying to have a child of their own for five years with no success. After undergoing tests, the doctors had informed them that Kris's endometriosis was the likely cause of her infertility and that it was unlikely they would ever be able to have children. With each passing year, Kris and Andy became more and more discouraged. Finally, they began to investigate the potential of adopting a child. But then miraculously, God blessed Kris and Andy's marriage with the birth of a perfect little girl. They named her Ally and delightedly welcomed their precious bundle of joy into their lives.

With the recent expansion of her family, Kris felt totally content and at peace for the first time in years. Her life took on new meaning, with her very essence revolving around the needs of her little girl. While life had certainly become more hectic, Kris and Andy couldn't be happier. The days, weeks, and months seemed to fly by at an amazing pace. But somehow they always found the time to savor each moment, never once forgetting how blessed they were to have Ally in their lives.

Just short of her second birthday, Ally started exhibiting some strange symptoms: high fever, rash, strawberry tongue, red eyes, and swollen lymph nodes. At first the doctors were stymied as to what all these symptoms added up to. But then an alert pediatrician diagnosed Ally with an uncommon childhood illness called Kawasaki disease. Thankfully, because she was diagnosed early, Ally received the immunoglobulin she desperately needed to prevent serious damage to her heart. While Ally and her parents faced some difficult and trying months, the doctors assured Kris and Andy that their daughter would grow up to be a healthy young woman. Because of a speedy diagnosis and attentive care, their sweet baby girl was once again healthy.

Throughout the roller-coaster ride that Kris and Andy had taken with Ally, there was something nagging at the back of Kris's mind. She had noticed an unusual mole on her back, but with all the commotion and fear over Ally's health, Kris's concern over her own physical condition had taken a back seat. Kris pointed the mole out to her doctor on her next appointment. After carefully looking at it, he suggested a biopsy. It was then that the dominos began to fall. Just a few days after the mole was removed, Kris received an unexpected call from her doctor. The mole was malignant. She had melanoma.

Kris was confused and frightened. She questioned God: "You spared my baby's life—will you now take me in her place?" Kris rationalized that God couldn't possibly want her yet. It had taken too many years to be blessed with the birth of her daughter. Why would He choose to take her *now*, of all times?

Kris's first appointment with her oncologist was terrifying, to say the least. There would have been no possible way to prepare for the conversation that took place that day. Kris used every ounce of strength she had to stop herself from curling up in the corner and crying. She felt so cold and alone. Her doctor patiently explained all the treatment options to Kris and Andy. He was honest and kind, but he couldn't stop the concern from permeating his voice. Kris's mind swirled with turbulent emotions. She had a desperately hard time focusing. She wondered, "What did he just say? What is it that I have? What am I supposed to be doing?" She prayed that Andy was getting all of this down because she sure wasn't.

Once her head stopped spinning and the reality of her diagnosis began to take seed, Kris put her heart and soul into learning anything and everything she could about melanoma and its treatment. Based on what she learned, Kris and her husband opted for the most radical treatment plan possible. They decided that they were not going to take any chances; there was just too much at stake. Ally needed her mom, and Andy needed his wife for many years to come.

Kris underwent a resection and lymph node surgery. To her relief, the cancer was self-contained; it had not spread. Kris's doctor was optimistic that her aggressive treatment protocol provided a promising outlook for her future.

Nearly two years have passed since that fateful phone call. Since that time, Kris has had eight more moles removed. Of these, five were benign, while three were in the early stages of cancer. Kris understands that her fight against melanoma represents a lifetime of vigilance, but she is *so* thankful that God has given her a second chance to be the mom she so desperately wants to be.

. . .

Just as you do not know how the breath comes to the bones in the mother's womb, so you do not know the work of God, who makes everything.

—Ecclesiastes 11:5

God, we rejoice in the miracle of life . . . beautiful little babies who bring such joy to our lives. It is through these joys that we find the courage and strength we need to get through the difficult times in our lives. When our health fails us, please restore it and our faith in you so that we can once again celebrate life for all its goodness. Amen.

FIVE

Sweet Dreams

D IANE AND JOHN had been friends for most of their lives. They lived close, went to the same schools, played together as young children, and hung out—like best friends often do—as they grew older. What was really cool was that they were related–they were cousins.

When John was diagnosed with non-Hodgkin's lymphoma at the age of eighteen , Diane was there for him, helping him force this dreaded disease into remission. He rebounded with the strength of a healthy, young teenager and went on with his life as if nothing had ever happened.

When Diane was a junior in college, she was offered an incredible opportunity to study abroad. She relished the idea of exploring new horizons and making new friendships. Without hesitation, she seized the opportunity. As Diane and her parents began to pack the car for their journey to the airport, John came jogging down the street. He ran up to Diane and pulled her into a fierce embrace, telling her he would miss her. Both agreed to stay in touch and to write often. As Diane and her family drove off, her eyes began to mist. With the frenzy of activities needed to prepare for her trip, she hadn't thought about John. Now it hit her. She was going to study in Italy with a bunch of strangers she didn't even know . . . and she wouldn't have John with her. She realized then how much she was going to miss him.

Living in Italy turned out to be an everyday adventure that left little time for Diane to be bored or to labor over those she had left behind. She became immersed in her studies and began to refine her Italian speaking skills. Di met many new people and toured Europe whenever the opportunity presented itself. While she missed those at home, she found herself adapting to her new life in Italy quite well. She would have so many things to tell them all when she came home the following summer.

That Christmas, Diane's parents called to tell her that John's lymphoma had returned. Di was saddened by the news, but she put her faith in John's doctors. They had cured him once before; she was confident they would do it again. Diane was twenty-one years old and surprisingly naïve; she still believed that death was reserved for old people. She never completely understood how life-threatening John's illness was. So when Diane's parents called her in February and told her that John had passed away, she came unglued. All at once, Italy felt like a prison for Diane. It held her from her family and friends . . . and John. She went to visit the university's priest–who was, ironically, named Father John. But he did not provide the comfort and help that only her John could provide. Beaten and depressed, Di headed back to her dormitory. She laid her head on the pillow that gloomy afternoon and sunk into a deep, deep sleep.

Diane began to dream. The dream was so incredibly real that, at first, she couldn't tell if she was asleep or awake. She concentrated with all her might, but she couldn't see anything. Then off to the left, a dim light began to glow, rapidly gaining in intensity. Suddenly an image started to form in Diane's mind. She could see a disco ball glittering and spinning, with light radiating from beneath. There was a woman, full of high-spirited energy, dancing without a care in the world. Diane looked intensely at the woman and was surprised to discover that she was looking at herself. She watched herself excitedly yell out to everyone, "Hey, everybody, he's here! John is here!" Then she skipped off the stage, stepping back into complete darkness. At once, the dreamer and the actor in the dream merged into one person . . . Diane was herself.

As Di looked ahead, the outline of two large gates began to crystallize. Soft golden light radiated from the gates, inviting her to step closer. As she did so, the gates began to open as if by magic. Suddenly, ten to twelve young men appeared in front of the gate. All were smiling bright, sunny smiles. Diane moved close enough so that she could see the features on each of their faces, the colors of their eyes, the styles of their haircuts, the shapes of their mouths. As her gaze wandered from man to man, her eyes were drawn to the center. There was John–her John! Diane thought, "John is alive!" Slowly, the young men began to disappear until only one was left standing–John. He gazed upon Diane, radiating warmth, love, and happiness. With a kind and gentle voice, he said, "Diane, I'm OK. I'm OK." Then he too faded away.

Diane awoke with a start, recalling the dream in vivid detail. She deliberated over the total look of peace she had seen on John's face and the light that had seemed to radiate from around his head. She found that the dream had been surprisingly soothing. She felt comforted and warmed, knowing that John had found a new home in heaven. The dream provided Diane with the sustenance she needed to finish her school year in Italy, before returning home the following summer.

When Diane was diagnosed with breast cancer several years later, she thought of John and remembered the peace she had felt within that dream. Throughout the year, she constantly felt John at her side and knew he was watching over her.

For more than twenty years, Di kept her dream to herself, sharing it with no one. Then one afternoon, she attended a shower for a cousin. As she stood at the party, she suddenly felt an urge to turn and gaze across the room. There she saw Arlene, John's mother, looking at her intently. Diane made her way through the crowd and stood before Arlene. They embraced. Instantly, Diane knew it was time to share her long-kept secret with her aunt. She looked Arlene in the eye and said, "I have something to tell you about John. I've kept it inside for the past twenty years because I was afraid to tell you." Arlene looked at Diane with concern and asked, "Did John hurt you?" Diane reassured John's mom with a pat on her arm, "No. No, it's not like that. He helped me when I had cancer. It's a good story. Can I share it with you?" Arlene answered, "Yes, please."

Diane revealed the mystery of her dream to Arlene. She finished the story and hugged her tightly, not wanting to let Arlene go. Many unspoken words and emotions passed between the two women with that one hug. As Arlene gently pulled away, she looked at Diane and said, "The day John died, I was the closest I *ever* was to God. I always felt like He had come down and took John up to heaven with Him. Thank you for sharing your dream with me, Diane. Today you have made my day . . . maybe even my life." The tears streamed down both of their faces as they embraced each other. Together they vowed to keep John's spirit alive in their hearts and minds forever.

. . .

In the last days it will be, God declares, that I will pour out my Spirit upon all flesh, and your sons and your daughters shall prophesy, and your young men shall see visions, and your old men shall dream dreams.

—Acts 2:17

Dear God, it is difficult to deal with the death of someone we have loved all our lives. We need to believe, on the basis of faith alone, that they will find peace and tranquility on the other side. Then, you send us a message. In our dream, all is well, and when we awaken, we know that our loved one is with you in heaven. Thank you for allowing us to dream wonderful dreams. Amen.

SIX

The Unanswered Prayer

DON WAS ENJOYING HIS MORNING COFFEE while working on his crossword puzzle. Now that he was retired, he had settled into a comfortable daily routine. His days were quite predictable, with very few surprises. That was how he liked it.

But today would be an "out of the ordinary" day for Don because he had scheduled a visit to the doctor for later in the morning. Don had invited his wife, Mary, to come with him. He'd take her out for a nice lunch afterwards, turning the appointment into a special outing. Truth be known, Don and Mary looked forward to getting out of the house for the day.

They arrived at the doctor's office a few minutes early. They'd been going to the same doctor for many years, so they knew the receptionist and nurses well. They joked around with everyone, enjoying the camaraderie as they did every time they visited. Everyone thought they were such a wonderful couple. They had been married for fifty-five years and were still so obviously in love.

Don flew through the exam, chatting amiably with his doctor. As they wrapped things up, Dr. Mishich told Don his PSA counts were very high, suggesting that something may be slightly off kilter with his prostate. The doctor explained that while it wasn't an assurance of prostate cancer, it was one of the markers that the medical community had come to rely on as an early warning sign.

Don had been healthy all his life and cancer did not run in his family. In fact, no one in his family had ever had cancer before. He shuddered to think that he might be the first . . . especially at the ripe old age of eighty-two. When Don and Mary told their children, Diane, Pat, Bob, and Sue, they were immediately concerned. While each prayed in their own way, the essence of their prayers was the same, "Lord, please don't let Dad have prostate cancer."

Unfortunately, subsequent tests dashed their hopes. The biopsy came back positive for cancer. In order to retard its growth, Don would have radiation seeds implanted in his prostate. Dr. Mishich assured him that he would be allowed to live a fairly normal life, with little pain or discomfort. While the family's prayers had not been answered, Don's family was nonetheless relieved that the cancer had been caught early and that his outlook was so promising.

As normal procedure dictates, the doctor ordered additional diagnostic tests to see if the cancer had spread. To the shock of all, the scan revealed a spot on one of Don's kidneys. A subsequent biopsy revealed that the kidney tumor had not metastasized from his prostate; instead, it was a separate and wholly unrelated type of cancer. Although it was in its absolute infancy, it required immediate and aggressive treatment. Left untouched, it was most certainly deadly. Doctors speculated that it was unlikely that the kidney cancer would have been discovered in time to successfully treat it . . . if it hadn't been for the prostate cancer. The prostate cancer had, in effect, saved his life.

Afterward, Don and his family thought back to all of their unanswered prayers. They had asked God to spare him from cancer, but their prayers had not been fulfilled. It was then that they came to realize that sometimes God doesn't respond to our prayers for a reason. He sees things that we cannot possibly see. Only He truly understands how everything fits together into His master plan.

. . .

Who among all these does not know that the hand of the Lord has done this? In his hand is the life of every living thing and the breath of every human being.

—Job 12:9–10

Dear God, sometimes we are upset when you do not answer our prayers. We feel that you have let us down or failed us. Please provide us with the strength and courage we need to trust you completely, without doubt. Help us understand that sometimes our prayers are left unanswered for a greater good that is not immediately known to us. Amen.

SEVEN

The Innocence of Youth

☙

P AT WAS THE THIRD PERSON in her church to be diagnosed with cancer in the short span of a year. The church members before her had lost their battles with cancer, passing away at forty-two and forty-nine years of age. These were the only two experiences with cancer that her children had ever had.

When she was told she had cancer, Pat and her husband, Frank, made the decision they thought was right for their family. They decided to tell Koreen (age 13), Rachel (age 11), and Jimmy (age 8) that Mom had a disease called Hodgkin's. It was a serious illness, but really quite curable. They explained that Mom might not be feeling too well for most of the year, but they'd get through it together. Everyone would pitch in and help out, and in the end, Mom was going to be all right. Pat and Frank diligently avoided all mention of the "C" word. They believed it was their responsibility to protect their children from harm's way. By doing this, they would spare them the anxiety of worrying about their mom dying . . . when it wasn't going to happen anyway.

Pat was a Sunday School teacher for a classroom of several young children, ages nine to eleven. She had sent a personal letter to all the parents of her students, advising them of her illness. She told them she had every intention of continuing to teach, but wanted their help in explaining the situation to their children. Pat knew she wouldn't always look or feel very good. She also recognized there would come a day when she would lose her hair. If the parents talked to their children, it would ease the journey for everyone.

What Pat could never have anticipated was that the grandmother of one of her students, Casey, had died of Hodgkin's. She had died thirty years earlier when cure rates were dismal, but under the circumstances, that didn't seem to matter. Casey showed up at the next Sunday School class and solemnly approached Pat, saying, "I am sorry you have cancer." Pat's daughter, Rachel, leaped to her defense, telling him, "She doesn't have cancer. She has Hodgkin's." Casey followed up with, "But Rachel, Hodgkin's *is* cancer." He then proceeded to tell the entire class that his grandmother had died of Hodgkin's. Pat's heart sank. She now had to work damage control with her own children . . . and fast.

After church, Pat and Frank sat down with their children and explained that Mom had cancer. They reassured them that it wasn't aggressive or deadly like the cancer the other church members had experienced. They explained that, while the year would be a tough one, Mommy would battle the cancer and win. They asked Koreen, Rachel, and Jimmy for their love, prayers, and help.

Contrary to what they had anticipated, Pat and Frank were totally surprised by how well their children reacted to the news. They didn't seem to share the fear of their parents. Maybe it was because in their short lives, they had never had to face anything quite this challenging. Maybe they just knew that God wouldn't take their mom from them. Maybe, like kids, they were just "living in the moment." Regardless of the reason, the children were amazingly supportive. Each child hugged and kissed their mom and told her she would be fine. They told her they would help out around the house and would include her in their evening prayers.

This experience taught Pat and Frank a valuable lesson—it's better to be upfront and honest with your children. Children model themselves to behave and act like their parents. While Pat and Frank's intentions were good, they were not being totally honest, nor were they giving Koreen, Rachel, and Jimmy enough credit. Their children proved to be far more capable of handling the news than Pat and Frank ever thought possible.

As time wore on, Pat found it was much easier to fight the cancer with her children "in the know." Everyone in her family pulled together to achieve the same goal. On down days, they would lie next to Pat in bed, reading her stories or rubbing her back. On significant days in her treatment plan, she would come home to handmade posters, banners, and balloons telling her how proud they were of what she had accomplished. On her birthday, they wrote her a special song and sang it with sweet and tender voices. On the last day of treatment, they all waited anxiously for Pat to come home from the hospital to celebrate the beginning of the next chapter in her life.

Occasionally, over the course of that year, people would commiserate with Pat, commenting on how difficult it must have been to have three young children to care for while having to deal with cancer. But Pat never agreed with them; instead, she felt exactly the opposite. Looking back, she doesn't know how she would ever have made it through that year without their good cheer, their encouragement, and their giggles.

Pat believes her battle with cancer ultimately had a positive effect on her children. Looking at them several years later, she believes they are more tolerant of people going through difficult times. They don't seem to take good health for granted as so many other children do. They are advocates for cancer-related fund-raising events in their school classrooms, at church, and in their community. They understand that family, friends, and God can make a difference in their lives and the lives of others. While this may have been a difficult year for them, it also represented a defining year; a year that will likely encourage them to be better siblings, spouses, friends, and parents in the years to come.

. . .

Our steps are made firm by the Lord, when he delights in our way; though we stumble, we shall not fall headlong, for the Lord holds us by the hand.

—Psalm 37:23–24

Dear God, please help us select the right path when encountering difficult choices in our lives. If we err and choose the wrong one, please redirect us so that we may fulfill your greater purpose. Thank you for all the children of the world. Their innocence renews us, encouraging us to appreciate each moment of our lives for what it is—a gift from you. Amen.

EIGHT

Visualizing a Cure

S ANDY'S LIFE HAD BEEN in a constant state of turmoil since that heart-breaking day when she had been told she had cancer. She had not had one moment of peace since. Not one single, solitary moment. Her mind raced steadily back and forth, always coming back to the same thought: *I have cancer!* Every waking minute of every day, she thought about her cancer. It was so hard to understand. One day she was living a normal life; the next, she was catapulted into a world dominated by cancer and all the horrors associated with it. It was nearly unbearable.

As she struggled to cope with her ever-racing thoughts, Sandy shared her fears with her nurse, Brittney. Brittney talked to her about visualization–a technique that she suggested could help to calm her mind. Using some type of imaginary device, Sandy could help focus her brain to destroy the cancer lurking in her body and, at the same time, potentially find some sense of peace.

Sandy read everything she could on visualization, becoming a firm believer in the process. She felt that if an average human being uses less than 10% of the brain, why couldn't it be believable that by using just a little more, one could focus the brain to help in the healing process?

After trying numerous visualization techniques that failed, Sandy finally stumbled on one that worked for her . . . sunshine. She *loved* sunshine. Its rays had always been successful in warming her body, soul, and mind. She began to visualize the cancer as a solid, black mass within her chest. She would then swallow an imaginary ball of glowing sunshine and visually bounce this ball off the cancer, slowly chipping away at its absolute blackness, over and over again.

Undeniably, it was difficult for Sandy. She wasn't the kind of person who relaxed very well. She was always up and moving, often doing two or three things at the same time. So at first, Sandy could only visualize for five to ten seconds before losing focus. She found it extremely challenging and exhausting to concentrate that fully on *one* thing, completely shutting out the world around her. But over time, with practice, the technique became easier and more comfortable. Finally, Sandy found success and was able to visualize for up to twenty minutes at a time, depending on her needs.

Sandy used visualization during all of her treatments and tests. She visualized the drugs being injected into her body as an infusion of pure, blinding sunlight designed to chip away at the cancer, eliminating it from her body. She visualized the radiation as beams of bright sunlight repeatedly penetrating her body, burning holes through the cancerous black mass. During tests, she visualized the total absence of any darkness within her body.

Sandy finished her chemotherapy and began radiation. On the day of her sixth treatment, she was, as usual, visualizing the sunlight penetrating the core of her cancer. But on this particular day, a daunting thing happened. The ray of sunlight that entered her body shot right out her back. "What the heck?" she thought. Within seconds her mind wrapped around what had just happened, and she realized that her cancer was gone. When the technicians entered the room, she looked up at them with obvious delight and said, "The cancer is gone!" She expected their chuckles or, at the very least, their total dismissal of what she had just said. But instead, when she explained what had happened, they agreed that the cancer was indeed gone. Over the years, they had learned to believe and trust in the power of visualization, because they had experienced its success firsthand.

Years later, Sandy continues to use visualization when she goes back to the hospital for periodic testing. But today she always visualizes the rays shooting right out her back. The cancer has never returned.

. . .

The human mind plans the way, but the Lord directs the steps.

—Proverbs 16:9

Dear God, while we know that you are by our side, we also understand that we must help you work your wondrous deeds. Please grant us the wisdom and courage we need to exercise the talents you have given us. Amen.

NINE

Renewed in Life and Love

❦

I T WAS A TYPICALLY BRIGHT AND SUNNY springtime day in Arizona. The birds were chirping, the desert blossoms were in full bloom, and the mountains stood majestically in the background. It was hard to find fault with anything in Tucson that day.

But Mike's disposition that March day was anything but sunny. He was sitting in his doctor's office desperately trying to absorb the full impact of the words that he had just heard. Mike's doctor had confirmed that not only was the tumor in his neck cancerous, but Mike had throat cancer. The doctor's words were droning on and on into one incomprehensible monologue. Mike heard snatches of his conversation . . . "more tests," "surgery," "radiation," "chemotherapy." These were words that Mike had heard before, in different conversations and different times, but never before had they been directed at him. All of a sudden, one short phrase grabbed Mike's attention, pulling him out of his daydream, "You have a small chance of survival."

Mike's thoughts strayed to his lovely wife, Mindy. He began to wonder, "How long do I have left? How can I tell Mindy?" Before he realized it, Mike was in his car on the journey home. As he drove, his thoughts kept drifting back to Mindy. The more he thought about telling her, the more emotional he became. His eyes misted over as he began to comprehend just how much this was going to hurt her. He could deal with the news the doctor had just presented to him—but he wasn't sure that Mindy could.

Two days passed, and still Mike had not yet summoned up enough courage to share his grave news with Mindy. Finally, late in the afternoon of the third day, Mike met Mindy at the door as she returned home from work. With an unsteady voice and a heavy heart, he asked her to sit down. Without a word, Mindy knew something was terribly wrong. Mike held Mindy's hand and looked her in the eye. "Mindy, I have some news I don't think you are going to want to hear . . . I have cancer." Mike filled her in on all the details, complete with his predicted poor prognosis. Mindy sat in shock, with a stunned and vacant look on her face. She sat silently, without moving, for a long time. Then she began to come alive, sputtering words of disbelief, wearing her raw emotions on her sleeve. At first it looked as if she would lose total control. But then, astoundingly, she drew in a deep and cleansing breath and summoned strength from deep within her inner being. She sat up straighter, courageously lifted her chin, and leveled a passionate gaze at Mike. "We are going to beat this, Mike. You are going to be OK. I am not going to lose you." And so the journey began.

Following that conversation, the clouds began to clear and Mike's perspective changed. He felt Mindy's strength seep into his very heart and soul. For the first time since his diagnosis, Mike found the power to face his mortality, confronting it head-on. He was no longer alone. He was no longer afraid. He had Mindy.

Mindy became integrally involved from the get-go. She organized a search to locate the best oncologist in town. She sat with Mike through all of his tests. She waited expectantly with him before and after surgery. When radiation began, Mike's throat became so damaged that he had difficulty swallowing. Mindy shopped for special foods and drinks that she thought Mike might be able to handle. Day after relentless day, she pushed Mike to his limits. When he was consumed with the negative things happening in his life, Mindy continuously found the positives all around him, constantly encouraging him and lifting his spirits. When Mike became frustrated with the horrors of what he was going through, Mindy reassured him that he was doing a great job and that she was immensely proud of him. At random times throughout the day Mindy called Mike, pushing him to eat and encouraging him to keep up the good fight.

At last, Mike's treatments were completed. Doctors were confident that the cancer was gone. But rather than feeling good, Mike found that his health continued to deteriorate. His throat was so damaged that he couldn't eat or drink, and the excess weight started to melt off Mike's body. The more weight he lost, the weaker he felt. As he lay crushed and shrunken in the bedroom of his and Mindy's home, he began to feel a sense of dread. Mike felt as if the end were near; in fact, he almost welcomed it. He was tired of fighting. But Mindy kept up the fight on Mike's behalf. She found a drink loaded with nutritional supplements that would help Mike's body heal itself. She encouraged him to drink just *one* bottle. She sat by his side, prodding and cajoling him until, at last, Mike had no choice but to drink what Mindy was trying to force into his body. It took almost all the effort he could muster to finish that first bottle, but at last he did. Mindy was ecstatic. "You did it, Mike. You did it, Honey!" Encouraged by Mindy's positive words, Mike forced himself to drink more and more cans each day. Finally, one day, he downed six cans while Mindy was at work. Terribly proud of himself, he called Mindy at the office and excitedly shared his news. "Min, I just finished my *sixth* can!' Mindy's voice cracked on the other end of the phone as she told Mike how proud she was of him. Mike sighed with contentment. Mindy had pulled him through a darkness he had never dreamed he would come to know.

A few months later, Mike and Mindy took a trip to Maui. The stage was set for romance. The island was stunning . . . beautiful beyond words. Mike and Mindy took sunset walks on the beach and talked romantically about their future life together. Once, their future had seemed uncertain; now it held great promise. On the evening of their twentieth wedding anniversary, during a special ceremony on a Maui beach at sunset, Mike and Mindy renewed their wedding vows. The ceremony represented a spiritual and healing event for both of them. On that evening, Mike came to realize that not only had he and Mindy just renewed their vows, but that he had renewed his love for his wife. He gazed upon the lovely, giving face of his wife and realized that her strength and love had provided him with the spirit he had needed to defy the odds.

. . .

Love is patient; love is kind; love is not envious or boastful or arrogant or rude. It does not insist on its way; it is not irritable or resentful; it does not rejoice in wrongdoing, but rejoices in the truth. It bears all things, believes all things, hopes all things, endures all things.

—1 Corinthians 13:4–7

Dear God, we thank you for gracing our lives with special people that make such a difference. They seem to know just when a kind word, a comforting shoulder, or a gentle push is needed. Our lives would not be the same without their loving touch. Our lives would not be the same without your love. Amen.

TEN

Miles Apart

M ARY, JOHN, AND LAURA WERE A FAMILY. It was just the three of them; it had started that way, and there was a sense that it would end that way. But Mary and John knew that one day soon their little girl would mature into a young woman and would have to make her own life. They also recognized that her path might be different than the one they had chosen. They were resolved to encourage Laura to spread her wings and fly when that time came.

The years flew by, and soon it was time for Laura to move on. When she decided to enroll in a college on the other side of the state, Mary and John accepted her decision with grace and dignity. Mary didn't have a driver's license, and John found the long drive far too fatiguing, so visits back home fell exclusively on Laura's shoulders. Burdened with a heavy class schedule, those visits became few and far between. The family relied on phone calls to stay in touch and rejoiced on holidays and during summer months when Laura spent valuable and much-appreciated time at home with her parents.

When Laura graduated from college four years later, she found a great job in the city where she had gone to school. With the acceptance of this job came Laura's decision to start her own life as an adult, five hours away from home. Mary and John were pleased with Laura's new opportunity. They realized that this was what they had trained her to do, to live her own life. But just the same, they were sad that their only child was settling so many miles away from home. While only 300 miles away, with no easy way for them to visit, it might as well have been 300 *thousand* miles.

Laura's career blossomed. She met the love of her life and married. As Laura's new life placed increasingly greater demands on her available time, her visits back to Albany occurred less and less frequently. But still, Laura remained close to her parents, talking by phone on a weekly basis and staying current on all the major events taking place in their lives.

Then Laura and Mike presented a gift to John and Mary that was a dream come true–an adorable little girl, named Katie. John and Mary were grandparents for the first time; they couldn't have been more thrilled. In their eyes, the sun rose and set on Katie. They swelled with pride and admiration for the latest addition to their family.

Two careers and a lively little baby only served to widen the miles between Laura and her parents. Katie didn't travel well, fussing most of the journey. So a five-hour drive with her was nothing short of exhausting. As a direct result, trips back home became a rarity. Although Laura and Mike wanted Katie to know her grandparents well, they rationalized that there would be plenty of time later . . . when Katie was just a touch older and a bit easier to travel with.

While Laura and Mike's life moved along at a rapid pace, John and Mary's had started to head down a slightly different and shaky path. The textile mill that John had worked at for thirty-five years suddenly and unexpectedly closed their doors, moving their operations to Mexico. John was devastated, for this was the only career he had ever known. But he decided to be as positive as possible about this recent change in his life. He enrolled in computer classes at the local community college in an attempt to learn a new skill and make himself more marketable. In a way, he thought it might be kind of fun and he welcomed the challenge.

But shortly thereafter, John began to experience cardiac problems. He underwent an angioplasty and, unfortunately, needed to put his plans for schooling on hold. John and Mary were forced to slow the pace of their lives down. To add insult to injury, John began to experience severe back pain. His body already racked with arthritis, he worried that his condition had progressed to rheumatoid arthritis. While he was frightened to confirm his suspicions, at the same time he was desperate to alleviate his pain. So he visited his family doctor . . . something he typically avoided at *all* costs. John underwent a barrage of tests to help pinpoint the cause of his back pain.

Then came the shocking news. It wasn't rheumatoid arthritis at all. It was something far worse. John had cancer. It was originally thought to be bone cancer, but the doctors later concluded that the primary site of the cancer was a tumor on his lungs. Left untreated, the cancer had metastasized to his spine, leaving John with a very grim outlook and an intense amount of pain.

The phone call that Laura received from her mother that day rocked her to the very core. She tried to reassure her mom, telling her that cancer is not nearly as deadly as it used to be and that people survive even the worst types of cancer. She soothed her by saying, "Mom, we can't give up hope. We can *never* give up hope." Truth be known, Laura was reassuring herself as much as her mother as she passionately spoke those words of encouragement.

John began his treatment with his wife by his side. Laura's career and her busy life with her husband and baby kept her miles away from Albany. She talked to her father every chance she got and received ongoing progress reports from her mother. She felt confident that her father was receiving the best possible care and that his doctors were doing all they could to try to destroy the cancer in his body. Laura constantly kept her father in her daily thoughts, praying fervently for his recovery.

Time slowly dragged on. John spent one long year enduring the pain and discomfort of chemotherapy and radiation. While the therapy had initially stopped the progression of the cancer, eventually it seemed to lose its potency. John's health once again began to deteriorate, causing the doctors to give up hope. They recommended that he go home and rest peacefully, with his family by his side.

Mary called Laura and told her the disturbing news. In her pain and anguish, she challenged Laura, "Where have you been? Why hasn't Katie come to visit her grandpa?" Laura had a difficult time explaining that it was just too difficult to simultaneously deal with her father's worsening condition *and* the demands of an energetic one-and-a-half year-old. The only way to remain sane was to compartmentalize the two and deal with each separately. Plus, Laura told herself, this was *not* how she wanted her daughter to remember her grandfather.

Mary insisted that Laura come home immediately. Laura knew her mother was not one to overreact. If many believed it was time to come home, Laura knew it was time to go home. The five-hour drive to her parents' house was the longest and loneliest journey of Laura's life. She was torn between feelings of guilt and sadness and she felt as if her life was careening out of control. The tears streaked down her cheeks. At times they nearly blurred her vision as she struggled to arrive home safely.

When Laura finally reached home, her dad was lucid and alert. He was *so* happy to have his daughter home, at long last. He was unusually euphoric, chatting amiably with all the relatives and friends who came that day to pay their respects. Laura spent several wonderful hours with her father before she and her mother said good night for the evening. She rested somewhat peacefully that night, sustained by her pleasant conversations with her father. He seemed to be doing *so* well. But the very next day, John slipped into a coma, never to reach a state of consciousness again. It was almost as if he had waited for his Laura to come home before he chose to give up the fight.

As John lay in his coma, Laura sat frozen by her father's side, devoid of all feeling. This wasn't her father. This was not the man she wanted to remember. John was usually energetic and full of life. He was a man who was never at a loss for words. But now he lay in his bed, silent and motionless. Laura sat in shock. Even the tears refused to fall. As she stared at her father, she began to realize that the essence of who he was–his personality, his charm, his intellect–was gone. Then she remembered something her father had once shared with her. He had told her that your physical body is merely a vessel for your soul; it doesn't represent who you are. Although this memory reassured Laura, she still felt totally empty inside. It wasn't until her husband and little Katie arrived that Laura's emotions began to resurface. With their entrance came life. With Katie's innocence came a sense of joy for mother and grandmother alike.

Now that her father has been gone for several years, Laura sometimes wonders if she handled things the way she should have. She questions if she should have taken Katie all those miles to see her grandfather, even as his body and mind slipped from this world. But when she looks at her daughter, she constantly reassures herself that she made the right choice. For Katie's memories of her grandfather are shaped from the way he *lived* rather than from the way he died. Today, at six years of age, Katie looks at the picture of her grandma and grandpa on her nightstand and talks fondly of the grandpa she never knew. The vivid stories that her mother and grandmother have shared with her over the years have made Katie feel as if they happened to little Katie and Grandpa themselves. Katie understands that Grandpa is living a wonderful life in God's kingdom, not miles away, but only a prayer away.

. . .

For everything there is a season, and a time for every matter under heaven; a time to be born, and a time to die; a time to plant, and a time to pluck up what is planted; a time to kill, and a time to heal; a time to break down, and a time to build up; a time to weep, and a time to laugh; a time to mourn, and a time to dance.

—Ecclesiastes 3:1–4

Dear God, guilt is such an unproductive emotion. So often we let it consume us, eating away at our very essence. Yet we understand that it does nothing to help the situation. Please help us do the right thing at the right time so we can feel confidence, rather than guilt, when we look back on the decisions we have made in our lives. When we make choices that we later question, please show us the way to inner peace. Amen.

ELEVEN

The Greatest Gift of All

🔥

MIKE WAS TURNING forty in a month, and life couldn't be better. He was happily married to Pat and had a wonderful relationship with his ten-year-old son, Ryan. All in all, Mike seemed to be at the peak of his life.

Turning forty didn't bother Mike like it seemed to bother so many other men. As far as he was concerned, it was just another number. But Pat disagreed. She thought that reaching the pivotal age of forty was a slightly bigger deal. So she was planning a surprise birthday party to end all birthday parties. She had invited relatives and friends from miles away. Many hadn't seen Mike in years and couldn't wait for the party. But as far as Mike knew, it was business as usual.

When it came to his daily life, Mike was a creature of habit. Every year he visited his doctor for his annual physical. At the end of the visit he immediately set up his appointment for the following year. It wasn't that Mike had any health concerns or that there were any major genetic diseases in his family; it was actually just the opposite. Mike was a young, vibrant, and healthy forty-year-old man, and he wanted to keep it that way.

This year, when Mike completed his physical, he expected to hear the usual, "You're good for another 10,000 miles, Mike!" But instead, his doctor told him he had found a lump in one of his testicles and that he would have to undergo further tests. Without any complicated medical explanations, Mike instantly recognized that testicular cancer was one of the potential outcomes.

He drove home in complete silence, frantically trying to come to grips with the implications of what he had just been told. He wondered how he could possibly break this news to his wife. He entered their home quietly, still absent of the words he needed. But as it turned out, he did not need to say a single word. Pat had been an integral part of Mike's life for so many years that she didn't need spoken words to understand that something was dreadfully wrong. She read the fear all over her husband's face and instantly asked, "Mike, what's wrong?" Mike hesitantly shared his news with her, while she gently held him, reassuring him that they would get through this together, as a team.

Mike and Pat were forced to wait several days before his scheduled appointment with the urologist. The days dragged, with both pondering every potential fear and pitfall imaginable. Sunday dawned, and they headed to church, like every other Sunday. They were hopeful that the sense of community they felt at their church would help to replenish their diminishing reserve of courage. And like so many other times in their lives, God answered their heartfelt prayers.

One of their church's members happened to be a physician, as well as a good friend. When he noticed the vacant and desperate look in their eyes, he recognized the expression immediately. It was the look borne by his patients when he delivered news they didn't want to hear. On instinct alone, Jim approached them and offered his assistance. The trio went to a quiet, private room where he gently prodded them to share their story. He answered their questions and told them what to expect. His knowledge and confidence reassured Mike and Pat, and they discovered that added reserve of courage they had so desperately been looking for.

Monday morning dawned, as did the pending doom and gloom of visiting the urologist. As they nervously waited for Dr. Brandenburg, Pat and Mike held hands, drawing strength from each other's touch. The doctor entered the room briskly and, without mincing words, laid it all on the line. "Mike, it is *very* likely that you have testicular cancer."

The surgery was scheduled for one week later. Mike wanted to take a little time to get things in order at work and to plan for his medical leave of absence. Early detection and Mike's annual physical had worked in his favor, allowing him to take the time he needed instead of being rushed to surgery.

Meanwhile, Pat was struggling with her own internal debate. The surprise fortieth birthday party that she had painstakingly planned for months was just five days away. She wondered in light of this disturbing news whether she should cancel the party. She was paralyzed with indecision and finally decided to turn to her family for advice. They thought the party was the best possible gift that Pat could offer to Mike. He could recharge his batteries by basking in all the love and support that his family members and close friends would offer him. It would help take his mind off the pending surgery, if only for a short time. So Pat bravely moved forward with her plans.

On Saturday morning, just three short days before his surgery, Mike arrived at a hall for what was supposed to be a couple's wedding shower for some very dear friends. To his amazement, 125 family members and friends greeted *him*, yelling, "Surprise!" Mike ate, danced, and sang songs that lifted his heart and his spirits. Memories of days gone by were shared from person to person. These newly created memories were being stored away for safekeeping, to be taken out and remembered when times got tough in the days, weeks, and months to follow.

News of Mike's pending diagnosis spread quickly. While at first it felt a bit uncomfortable for Pat and Mike, their discomfort soon dissipated as treasured family and friends offered words of encouragement, support, and love. Mike floated home at the end of the evening, lighthearted. He considered himself blessed that he had so many wonderful people in his life and that all these people cared so deeply for him.

On Sunday, Mike and Pat publicly shared their news at church during the Joys and Concerns section of worship. There weren't too many surprised faces—after all, many had been at the party the previous evening, and bad news travels fast. But there were more words of encouragement and plenty of promises for daily prayers for Mike. He indeed felt blessed to be surrounded by such a caring and loving church family.

As they drove home, Mike's thoughts strayed. Without intending to think about it, he pondered, "Only two more days until surgery." But unlike just a few short days earlier, when all Mike could do was think obsessively about what awaited him, he now felt calmed by his memories of the wonderful weekend he had shared with his family and friends. Even though he knew he was facing surgery and potential treatment for many months, he was flying higher than a kite. So many people had come to his party. Some had traveled many miles . . . *just for him*! Others—who had not seen him for fifteen years or more—had also shown up for the celebration. It was truly amazing.

So on Tuesday morning, Mike went to surgery *not* with a heavy heart, but with a heart filled with love, support, and hope. While the surgeon confirmed that Mike indeed had testicular cancer, there was no lymph node involvement and the tumor had not spread. That was great news.

During treatment, Mike's family and friends continued to offer encouragement in the form of phone calls, cards, prayers, and visits. One evening, a friend shared a video he had taped of the birthday party festivities with Mike and Pat—it provided a gift of love and laughter at a much-needed time in their lives.

As Mike and Pat reflect back on that time in their lives, fourteen years ago, they thank God for helping them face their deepest fears. He understood that they would be better equipped to handle their difficult journey if they were ensconced in the warmth and love of family and friends. Love conquered most of their fears, and the Lord helped them through the rest.

. . .

"Teacher, which commandment in the law is the greatest?" He said to him, "'You shall love the Lord your God with all your heart, and with all your soul, and with all your mind.' This is the greatest and first commandment. And a second is like it: 'You shall love your neighbor as yourself.' On these two commandments hang all the law and the prophets."

—Matthew 22:36–39

Dear God, you told us that love is the greatest gift of all and to love one another as you have loved us. We thank you for all the loved ones we have been blessed with in our lives. We praise you for knowing exactly when to have these special people intervene in our lives. Thank you for their love, as well as your everlasting love. Amen.

TWELVE

In the Public Eye

M ELODIE HAD NOT HAD A MOMENT of real peace for quite some time. Whenever anything happened in her professional or personal life, it was splashed all over the media. While she loved her career as an anchorwoman for one of the key local television stations, it was not without its moments.

Melodie was a wife and mother to four beautiful children: Morgan, Courtney, Lauren, and Ryan. She treasured each moment with her family, totally immersed in their everyday life, complete with its triumphs and disappointments. Melodie and her husband, Wayne, did what they could to protect their children from her public life, giving them as normal a childhood as possible.

Melodie was also a consummate professional, doing her job and doing it well. Ironically, that was all most people knew of her. Very few had ever had the opportunity to gaze into her real life and see what she valued most. Melodie was sometimes surprised when she discovered that so many in her viewing audience had a tendency to put her on a pedestal. She wondered, "Can't they see that I am just like them?" Just like them, she had good days and bad days, happy times and sad times, moments of sheer happiness and moments of cold desperation.

When Melodie was diagnosed with cancer, she was alarmed, confused, and saddened—just like anyone else that has the misfortune of hearing the words, "You have cancer." But Melodie's public life put a wrinkle in her diagnosis that couldn't be overlooked or brushed aside. Melodie and Wayne had a tough decision to make. They had to decide how to control the flow of her diagnosis to the press.

Melodie was scheduled for surgery on Monday. The doctors would be unsure of her ultimate diagnosis until they determined how far the cancer had spread, if at all. Without a thorough diagnosis in hand, Melodie and Wayne made two difficult, but well thought-out, decisions. First, they decided to explain the surgery to their children in as much detail as the minds of an eight-, seven-, five-, and one-year-old could comprehend. Second, they decided to personally select the journalist who would break Melodie's story, rationalizing that they could control the depth of information, as well as the timing of its release to the general public.

They sat down with their children, carefully explaining that Mommy was going into the hospital for surgery. Something bad had happened inside her body. Some of mommy's cells had gone bad and were growing into a big clump of bad cells. The doctors had decided that if they could remove these cells, Mommy would be fine. They went on to explain that what Mom had was not a germ or virus, so they couldn't catch it from her. Wayne gave each of the girls a special book. He explained, "Sometimes it's hard to ask Mom or me a tough or embarrassing question. These books can help you. Any time you have a question, write it down in your book and put it on my dresser. I will read it and then help you understand what is happening." Melodie and Wayne didn't use the word "cancer" when they spoke with their children—at this point in her diagnosis, they didn't think it was important to frighten them.

Melodie chose a journalist whose talent she respected to share her exclusive story with the public. She asked him to print the story the day after her surgery. The last thing she wanted was a trail of journalists following her as she left the hospital post-surgery. Thinking back, Melodie realizes that it was inevitable that the journalist speculated that someone would see her at the hospital on Monday and inform the media. If he honored Melodie's wishes, he'd miss out on his opportunity for an exclusive story. He would be scooped. Knowing that, he chose to break the story on Monday, while Melodie was in surgery.

Melodie and Wayne were unaware that her story was unfolding before the dazed and troubled faces of her viewers while she lay in surgery. It wasn't until much later in the day that they were shocked to see an in-depth story of her breast cancer diagnosis on the front page of the newspaper, above the fold, complete with a full-sized picture. The headlines screamed the news to all of Melodie's fans—*Melodie has breast cancer*! All the local television networks had also picked up the story. It was, after all, breaking news.

In the big scheme of things, the media's coverage of Melodie's plight was the least of her worries. Surgeons had discovered that her cancer was bigger and more aggressive than originally anticipated. Melodie and Wayne struggled to accept the diagnosis as it began to fully dawn on them how this was going to affect their lives.

Home from the hospital, Melodie knew it was time to re-brief the children on what the doctors had discovered and on what Mommy would have to go through in the months ahead. But she was tired and she was still absorbing the shock of the news herself. She wanted to gather her thoughts and to have Wayne by her side when she shared the news with them. So she made the decision to wait a few more hours until Wayne returned home.

Melodie occupied her time and thoughts with her daily tasks and chores, all the while turning over in her mind which words were the right ones to use with her children. She was an accomplished journalist. She had something to say on just about every topic. She was quite eloquent most of the time. She wondered, "Why now, when I so desperately need to explain something so critically important to my children, do I feel like I am at a loss for words?" But as fate would have it, there was no need to find the right words–the newspaper managed to take care of that just fine.

It happened at dinnertime. Ryan, Melodie's one-year-old, was in his high chair proudly feeding himself while the other children sat at the table eating dinner. All of a sudden, Ryan excitedly exclaimed, "Mommy!" Melodie looked over to see him pointing at the floor. She hurried over to Ryan's side to see what had dropped (or been thrown!) on the floor. To her amazement, she saw what he was animatedly pointing at . . . and so did her eight-year-old daughter, Morgan. It was a picture of Mommy, on the front page of the newspaper, complete with all the excruciating details of her breast cancer diagnosis. "Oh no," thought Melodie. This was *not* how she had intended to share the news with her children. Many emotions crossed her daughter's face–bewilderment, concern, anger, and then betrayal. It was this last emotion that tore at Melodie's heartstrings the most. It wasn't until later that evening that Melodie and Wayne learned the depth of Morgan's pain. The journal her father had given her showed up on his dresser. As they read what she had written, they were catapulted into the emotional chaos of Morgan's mind, "What is this? Is what the newspaper said true? Why didn't you tell me? What happens next?"

Melodie and Wayne were devastated. Not only were they struggling to accept the news themselves, they now also had to deal with the emotions churning through Morgan's mind. It was definitely time for damage control. Melodie and Wayne sat down first alone with Morgan, then later with their entire family. They explained they had wanted all the facts before they talked to the girls, so that they wouldn't worry. They described what chemotherapy was and what Mommy was going to go through. They helped to ease their fears, reassuring them that her diagnosis was promising.

Morgan accepted the calming words and hugs and kisses from her parents that evening, reassured that they would get through this as a family. While Morgan had been soothed, Melodie still worried about her ability at the innocent age of eight to deal with her mother having cancer. But God provided an earth angel for Morgan. Unknown to anybody at school, Morgan's third-grade teacher was a breast cancer survivor. Upon hearing the news, she immediately took Morgan under her wing. She ministered to her needs, answered her questions, and helped Morgan through the year with a never-ending supply of love and support.

As for that public life? Melodie is no longer a TV anchorwoman. She chose to use her firsthand knowledge of cancer, coupled with her local prowess, to create a local organization dedicated to helping breast cancer patients navigate the often-turbulent waters experienced after diagnosis. Melodie's program provides patients a mentor who had a similar diagnosis, as well as comparable interests and lifestyle choices. Together, the new and old patient make the difficult journey together.

. . .

But the Lord said to Samuel, "Do not look on his appearance, or the height of his stature, because I have rejected him; for the Lord does not see as mortals see; they look on the outward appearance, but the Lord looks on the heart."

—1 Samuel 16:7

Dear God, sometimes life doesn't go as planned. We're thrown a curve ball and struggle to deal with how it affects our lives. Just when we think we couldn't possibly handle more adversity, another problem knocks at our door. Please give us the strength to face these problems and the wisdom to know how best to deal with them. Provide us with just the right words at just the right time to help us make the right decisions in our lives. Amen.

THIRTEEN

An Rx for Healing

❦

D R. VENNE WAS AN ONCOLOGIST and a fine one at that. He had been trained at one of the finest medical schools in the country and had learned well. His opinion was regularly, sought and he had an impressive and long list of patients. Dr. Venne didn't consider himself to be a hero. He just did the best job he could each and every day.

Dr. Venne thought like a clinician because he was trained as a man of science. He explored all the known facts, made an educated and sound diagnosis, and took the necessary course of action to resolve the problem. He found amazing comfort in this constant chain of events.

That was why he found a request from the father of one of his patients so unsettling. Adam had been struck down at the height of his prime by a very aggressive acute leukemia. Initially he had tolerated chemotherapy well, but then had developed some severe complications. Adam's wife and young son watched in disbelief as the man they loved was now being kept alive by machines. Adam's father, Peter, had flown in from San Francisco to be by his son's side. When Dr. Venne entered the room, he rose, approached him, and asked him to do something that he believed would make all the difference in the world, "Doc, please pray for my son. I am sure God will listen."

Despite years of experience treating cancer patients, Dr. Venne had never received such a request on behalf of one of his patients. While he believed in God, he had always relied on science and medicine to heal his patients. He had never gone to God in prayer to ask for assistance and healing a hand.

Dr. Venne thought about Peter's request very seriously. Adam's family was very faithful; their reliance on God and God's goodness was a pivotal aspect of their lives. As Dr. Venne pondered, he questioned who *he* was to stand in the way of their beliefs. Right then and there, he made a decision to honor their request—not just privately, but in a more public way. Dr. Venne called a local Christian radio station and explained the situation. He asked the station and their listeners to include Adam and his family in their daily prayers. He also prayed for Adam himself.

Just three days later, Adam's condition showed dramatic and unexpected improvement. His progress was so significant that Adam was moved from the Intensive Care Unit to a regular hospital room. Adam's family thanked God for what they clearly saw as a miracle. Their unwavering testament to God's healing power gave Dr. Venne pause. Although this was not his first experience with a patient's spirituality, it was the first time he was able to be a part of that dimension of a patient's care. As he contemplated what had happened, he realized that physicians often forget that for many patients, the doctor's administering to their *spiritual* needs is often as critical as treating their *physical* needs.

Fueled by his success with Adam, as well as his own intellectual curiosity, Dr. Venne decided to research this issue to see if other physicians had experienced similar success stories. He discovered that over the past few years, reputable medical journals such as *The Journal of the National Cancer Institute* and the *International Journal of Aging and Human Development* had published articles specifically addressing the connection between spirituality and healing. Prestigious institutions, such as the Johns Hopkins University School of Medicine and Georgetown University, have integrated these aspects of healing into their training curriculum for new and upcoming physicians. These physicians are now being told that a patient's spirituality can indeed positively impact clinical outcomes.

Looking back, Dr. Venne recognizes that over many years and numerous interactions with countless faithful patients, he has been transformed himself. He no longer needs to turn to medical journals to confirm the healing power of God, for he has witnessed it firsthand.

Today, Dr. Venne invites patients and caregivers alike to explore this seldom addressed dimension of cancer treatment. He guarantees that it will enrich their lives in many unexpected ways. He himself now regularly prays for the recovery of his patients, skillfully blending science and faith together.

. . .

"Ask, and it will be given you; search, and you will find; knock, and the door will be opened for you. For everyone who asks receives, and everyone who searches finds, and for everyone who knocks, the door will be opened."

—Matthew 7:7–8

Dear God, we sense your greatness all around us and within us. We know that help is only a prayer away. We pray that you help others understand that your goodness can make a profound difference in their lives, as well as the lives of others. God, please bless all the medical professionals who help those with cancer, showing them the way and helping them understand that faith can indeed heal. Amen.

FOURTEEN

Don't Worry, Be Happy

✹

THE DAY HAD FINALLY ARRIVED. The *last* day of treatment! Shelly had dreamed of this day for over six months. No more radiation. No more chemotherapy. No more needles. No more sick hospital smells.

But after her last treatment, Shelly didn't feel like she had anticipated. In fact, she didn't feel anything at all like she had anticipated. She had expected to skip to the elevator at the hospital, full of energy, hope, and optimism. But instead, she dragged her body there, her face turned down in a grimace, her mind and heart heavy with sadness. She felt like she was moving through a wall of syrup, struggling to take even one step forward.

Today, like the other thirty-nine days of radiation, Shelly was alone. It had been her choice to be alone. She had purposely scheduled the treatments later in the day, with the thought that she would drive directly to the hospital from the office. When her treatment was done, she would make the short journey home. In her mind, it would have been hard to justify disrupting someone's life every day, Monday through Friday, for what amounted to a ten-minute appointment. So she had braved it alone.

When Shelly thought about it, it really hadn't been that bad. She had gotten to know Tiffany, the breast cancer patient who had treatment right before her, and Rachel, the ovarian cancer patient right after her. They had been soul mates of hers for this brief window of time. Each day, they shared their ongoing experiences with each other—their celebratory moments as well as their emotional crashes. They boosted each other's spirits as only soul mates could. Although they'd likely never see each other ever again, Shelly knew she'd always remember these special women in her life.

But today, on Shelly's last triumphant day, there was no one there to rejoice with her. Tiffany had finished her treatment a few days earlier and

Rachel was nowhere to be found. Shelly hoped that Rachel wasn't ill. Even Shelly's favorite radiation technicians, Peggy D. and Peggy K., were working a different shift. There was no one there to pat Shelly on the back, no one to tell her she was a hero. She was now a cancer survivor, but no one (not even Shelly) appeared to be overly elated about the event. She felt utterly alone.

So instead of jumping for joy, she found herself totally and completely depressed. She knew that, starting tomorrow, her life would be very different. No more daily trips to the hospital. No more discomfort or pain. No more cancer. Shelly just couldn't figure this one out. She thought, "Shouldn't I just be happy to be alive?" She knew that many people would happily trade places with her. "What the heck is wrong with me?" she chided herself.

But while Shelly was thrilled to be done with treatments, she knew that she was no longer actively doing something to make sure it didn't come back. Heck, she wasn't even sure if the cancer was really gone. Maybe it wasn't. She wasn't going to have her CT scans and blood work for several more weeks. Maybe they would still see a trace of the cancer in her body. Or maybe the cancer would start growing again. The more Shelly thought about these nagging concerns, the more depressed she became.

Weeks later, Shelly's CT confirmed that her cancer was indeed in remission. But somehow, she still continued to worry, asking herself over and over, "What if?" In three more months, she'd have tests again, but that felt like such a long time away.

Eventually, Shelly came to understand that she couldn't get through these emotions on her own. Inspired by conversations with her husband, Bill, Shelly began to realize that she needed to talk through her fears with someone who had been there, someone who truly understood her pain. So she joined a support group. She had previously thought that the kind of people who participated in support groups were weak . . . people who turned to others because they couldn't make it on their own. She had fancied herself far too strong and independent to commiserate with the likes of them. But Shelly came to realize just how totally mistaken she had been. The cancer patients and survivors in these groups were outgoing and positive. They used the support group as a way to connect with others who truly understood what they were going through. They welcomed current cancer patients to the group, guiding them through their questions, surgeries, medications, and treatment plans. As Shelly shared her emotional turmoil with cancer patients and survivors alike, she was reassured that the emotions she was feeling were totally normal. She had been fighting for her life for so long that when she no longer needed to focus on survival, she felt lost.

It began to dawn on Shelly that all the worry in the world wouldn't prevent the cancer from coming back . . . if it was going to come back. So she decided that rather than wasting away her waking hours with gnawing worry, she would embrace life for all its goodness and glory, rejoicing in each day God has made.

. . .

"So do not worry about tomorrow, for tomorrow will bring worries of its own. Today's trouble is enough for today."

—Matthew 6:34

God, we understand that worrying is a natural part of life, but know that it will not solve our problems. Yet sometimes we just can't seem to stop. Please fill us with the strength we need to put our complete faith and trust in you. You alone can make sure that our worst fears are not realized. Amen.

FIFTEEN

The Power of Love

❦

MARRIED THIRTY YEARS, Kathie and her husband, Tom, owned their own trucking business. They happily crisscrossed the United States in their semi, delivering paper products to customers and picking up produce for the journey home. Their son, Tom, and daughter, Brandee, were fully-grown and living productive, fulfilling lives of their own. Tom and Kathie felt like they had it all.

All the miles traveled together resulted in an even closer bond between Kathie and Tom. They relished their time together, whittling away the hours and making plans for their future. While content living their "empty nest" lifestyle, the daily life of a trucker can be tiring at times. So Kathie and Tom made sure to take frequent breaks and to spend as much time as possible at home. Regardless, fatigue settled in from time to time. So when Kathie first started to get just a little more tired than usual, she didn't worry. As is so often the case, she rationalized her fatigue away, trying to rest a little more often and to go to bed on a more regular schedule.

The fatigue continued despite Kathie's persistent efforts to get more rest. Then unexplained bruises began to appear on her legs. . . many bruises of different shapes and sizes. At the same time, Kathie's exhaustion heightened to the point where it started to adversely affect the quality of her life. Finally, the day came when she felt too weak to walk the short distance from their semi to a nearby restaurant. Both Kathie and Tom realized that a trip to the doctor was in order.

Kathleen's doctor was instantly concerned when he checked her over. He administered a number of blood tests, which ultimately led to a bone marrow biopsy. Kathie tried to think of the other positive things happening in her life rather than focusing on the difficult tests she was going through and the potentially bad results she might receive. She waited impatiently for her doctor's call. And then it finally happened—the phone rang. "Kathleen?" asked the voice on the other end of the phone. "Yes," Kathleen replied. "This is Dr. Mielke. I know you've been waiting for the results of your bone marrow biopsy. They just came today. (Several seconds of silence passed.) You have what is called acute myelogenous leukemia." Kathleen's thoughts churned through her brain. "What? Leukemia? How can that be? How could I have *that*?" Her brain raced, her pulse quickened, her concentration waned. Kathie couldn't speak. She couldn't breathe. If there were more important things that Dr. Mielke said, she missed them, for her mind was light years away.

When Tom heard the news, he was blown away. Never by any stretch of the imagination had he considered that Kathleen would be stricken with anything of this magnitude. He, like Kathie, had expected a diagnosis that could be easily cured with a few antibiotics and plenty of rest.

Ironically, this message had been delivered to Kathie on Good Friday. Remembering Jesus' death on that day, Kathie began to look at this day as the death of a chapter in her own life—the BC or "before cancer" phase. Whether she welcomed it or not, she was now in the AD or "after diagnosis" phase, and it surely was different than what had come before.

Kathie was immediately hospitalized. Her doctor implanted a port so that he could continuously feed chemotherapy drugs into her body, twenty-four hours a day, seven days a week. When Kathie experienced an allergic reaction to the drugs, they treated the burning, complete body rash and horrible itching, all while continuing to relentlessly pump the drugs into her body.

Kathleen completed her first round of treatment feeling weak, nauseated, bald, and very thin. Just when she started to feel quasi-human again, it was time for round two. On a positive note, during the second round it became apparent to Kathie and her doctor that the chemo *was* working. It was aggressively attacking the cancer cells. But unfortunately, at the same time, it was also killing many healthy parts of Kathie's body, including her much-needed bone marrow. The doctors informed her that she was left with two choices—she could find an eligible bone marrow donor and potentially survive or she could relish her remaining days with her family. Dr. Mielke told her that time was of the essence; she needed to make a decision and to make it quick. But Kathie need time to reflect, to pray, and to plan. She didn't think this was the kind of decision you made with the snap of your fingers.

In the end, the decision was easy. Kathie plainly and simply chose life. She was willing to search to the ends of the earth, if necessary, to find a matching bone marrow donor. But Kathie's search ended abruptly and effortlessly with her sister Karen. Never one to enjoy doctors or hospitals, Karen selflessly offered her bone marrow to Kathleen without a moment's hesitation.

As Kathie struggled to regain control of her life, her daughter, Brandee, became her biggest advocate. She was Kathie's voice when she was too sick or too weak to speak. She became her dad's office manager to keep their business running smoothly in her mom's absence. As Brandee selflessly gave of herself, a new life was forming inside of her, but she remained by her mother's side every step of the way, regardless of how fatigued or nauseated she herself felt.

Kathie's son, Tom, visited her frequently. He played games with Kathie to keep her mind alert and to inject some laughter into her life. He took her on short walks through the hospital, allowing her to experience life outside her hospital room. Tom stayed overnight often and watched over his mother, providing her with constant comfort and support. He was her protector.

Kathie's husband continued to run his trucking business throughout her illness. It was necessary to keep his insurance premiums current and to earn money to pay for the mounting hospital bills. Each trip back home found Tom at his wife's bedside, encouraging and rallying her to a speedy recovery. He terribly missed her on his cross-country treks and couldn't wait until they were reunited.

Kathie also had many other supporters backing her throughout her struggles. Her mother held the entire family together, wishing that she could carry this burden for her daughter. Her sister Barbara lived thousands of miles away but called each day for updates, offering words of encouragement and support. Her sister Karen's best friend, Sherry, sent cards and letters to Kathie every single day, despite the fact that she had never met Kathie. Kathie found herself on numerous prayer chains throughout her community and other communities. She felt so protected and loved. If she was ever alone, it was by her choice alone. Even then, she didn't feel alone, because the Lord was at her side.

One month after Kathleen left the hospital, in complete remission, Brandee gave birth to a beautiful baby boy they named Anthony. His birth reminded Kathie's family that life goes on. Anthony brought endless joy to Kathie and her family at a time when it was important to recognize the miracle of life and living. To this day, Grandma Kathie cherishes her grandson for all he represents to her–life, hope, and love.

. . .

"I give you a new commandment, that you love one another. Just as I have loved you, you also should love one another. By this everyone will know that you are my disciples, if you have love for one another."

—John 13:34–35

Dear God, sometimes we are asked to carry a difficult load. But at the same time, you offer us the love and support we need to make this load lighter. Thank you for surrounding us with so many people who love and care for us. With their love, we feel stronger, bolder, and more positive. With your love, we know that we can make it from one difficult day to the next, until finally our challenging days are ended and we are at peace. Amen.

SIXTEEN

The Battle between Good and Evil

R OSEMARIE FOUND HERSELF on the most unbelievable roller coaster ride of her life. She had just spent a gut-wrenching week visiting her sister, Barbara. Barbara had recently been diagnosed with stage 4 sarcoma and was gallantly fighting for her life. Each month, Rose flew north to help her through her chemotherapy, sitting at her hospital bedside, encouraging and praying with her.

Upon returning from her most recent trip, Rosemarie was forced to deal with yet another trying situation. Her relationship with Jim–her serious boyfriend of two years–had finally come to an impasse. Rose wanted to marry; Jim didn't. Fueled by Jim's fear of commitment and Rosemarie's sorrow and grief over her sister's imminent death, they chose to end their long-term relationship.

Now to add insult to injury, Rose had found a small lump in her breast. She chose to keep this news to herself for a while, too worried to voice her fears out loud. But finally, in desperation, she shared her news with her closest friends at work. They strongly encouraged her to go in and have the lump checked out. Rose knew they were right, but she was just so sick and tired of doctors and hospitals that she hesitated. Finally, her common sense prevailed, and she scheduled an appointment with her gynecologist.

The lump was small, so small that her doctor initially had trouble performing a needle biopsy. Because of its small size, no one was particularly concerned that it would amount to much of anything. As a result, Rose was not at all prepared for the news she received a few days later. The biopsy had confirmed that the lump was malignant. At first, the doctor assured Rose it was stage 1 breast cancer, caught in its infancy. But this diagnosis also proved to be false, as further tests reflected lymph node involvement and confirmed that Rose was HER-2 negative. Her doctor explained that she would need to undergo a lumpectomy, as well as rigorous chemotherapy and radiation treatments for the balance of the year.

Rose had been a very faithful person all her life. When she had prematurely buried her mother from complications with her diabetes, she had found solace in her faith. When a few years after moving to Arizona, her father had unexpectedly passed away, Rosemarie had prayed for inner peace and found comfort in her belief that her father had rejoined her mother in heaven. Again, when Barbara had been diagnosed with a very deadly form of cancer, Rose turned to prayer to help navigate the stormy waters she found herself immersed in. But her breakup with Jim, coupled with her own diagnosis of cancer, represented the straw that broke the proverbial camel's back. Rose was upset beyond words, fighting for control. She regaled at God, "How can you do this to me? Why have you poured so much hardship at my feet? First Barbara. Now me. Why? Why?" The anger consumed her waking thoughts, nearly paralyzing Rose.

Rosemarie was miserable beyond words. What little peace was present in her life, she found by cuddling up next to her dalmatian, George. George was her constant companion, protecting her from harm's way at all hours of the day and night. One evening, as Rose and George were out for stroll, they met her next-door neighbor Mark. Mark ran each evening, in line with the discipline engrained in him as a major in the U.S. Air Force. When he saw Rose, he slowed his run to a walk, amiably chatting with her until they arrived at her front door. They parted ways that evening, but spoke again in the future every time their paths crossed on the streets of their neighborhood.

Rose underwent a lumpectomy and began chemotherapy. Despite her pain and anguish over her own health, Rose still made her monthly pilgrimage to Wisconsin to take Barbara to the hospital for her treatments. She never thought of herself, but instead put the needs of her sister first.

With all the unexpected illnesses, Rose and Barbara's brother and sister thought it was time they get together as a family to celebrate their life and times together. They had selected the dates carefully, planning around both Rosemarie's and Barbara's chemotherapy treatments. The siblings and their families would travel from Florida, Wisconsin, and Arizona to be rejoined in Wyoming one last time before Barbara became too ill to travel. Rose was so excited. The thought of this reunion kept her stoically moving forward through her treatments with a sense of anticipation.

The morning that Rose was scheduled to leave for Wyoming, she awoke with an unusually high fever. She felt sick from head to toe. It was obvious that her immune system was in a shambles. Rosemarie's doctor vehemently banned any travel, telling her that she would put herself in grave danger if she chose to subject her body to all the germs present on the airplane. Rose broke down and cried for hours. She had depleted all of her emotional reserves. Never before in her life had she felt *so* completely alone. When she thought back on the whole of her life, all she saw was emptiness and loneliness. Both of her parents were gone; she no longer had Jim in her life; her sister was dying; and the rest of her family was celebrating in Wyoming . . . without her.

A few days later, Rosemarie's fever finally broke. Desperately needing a breath of fresh air, she leashed up George and headed outside. Just as on countless walks before, they saw Mark out on his nightly run. And just like before, he stopped to talk with Rose. Although Rosemarie was wearing a baseball hat, it was still obvious that she was bald. As the realization of this fact crept onto Mark's face, Rose exclaimed, "Mark, I have breast cancer." He instantly took her in his arms, reassuring her and making her promise to call if she needed anything . . . anything at all. The next morning, Rose opened her front door to find a bouquet of flowers with a card that said, "Rose–have faith in God. With His help, you will find the strength you need to get through this ordeal."

As time marched on, so did the predatory cancer lurking in Barbara's body. Her health continued to deteriorate, slowly oozing any sense of life from her body. Rose flew north immediately, holding Barbara close and comforting her. She helped to set up Barbara's home and to hire a hospice nurse so that Barbara could spend her last days in familiar and comfortable surroundings. As Barbara continued to fight with a vengeance, Rosemarie neared the day of her next chemotherapy treatment. She investigated the potential of having it administered in Milwaukee, but her doctor preferred that she come home to Tucson. So Rose flew home. One day after Rose arrived in Arizona, Barbara succumbed to cancer.

Rose wallowed in grief and pain in the privacy of her own home. George instantly knew something was wrong, cuddling up next to her, refusing to leave her side. He represented the bright spot in her otherwise miserable life. Just when Rosemarie didn't think she could endure one more moment of agony, the phone rang. "Hello," she mumbled. "Rose, this is Mark. I was wondering if you'd like to go out for ice cream with me." Rose said, "I don't think so, Mark. I wouldn't be very good company tonight." But Mark persisted until finally Rose gave in and joined him.

It didn't take long for Rose to spill every emotion she was feeling at Mark's feet. She pummeled him with her angry thoughts. "Why is God being so cruel to me? The man I love won't commit to me. I have breast cancer and still have six more months of treatment. The *one* opportunity I had to see my family and my dying sister was taken from me because I was too sick. I watched both of my parents suffer before they died, and now my sister is dead at the age of fifty. *What else can I bear?*"

Mark and Rose sat for three hours at the ice cream parlor that night, while she regaled him with tales of how angry she was with God. She told Mark, "I am a good person. I believe in God. I have faith. I am only forty-five, and yet my life has been filled with all this sorrow. So many of the people I have loved have died or left me. Why would God do this to me?" Mark absorbed what Rose said, being a patient and empathetic listener. When she had defused most of her pent up anger, he tried to calm Rose's raw nerves by saying, "God doesn't control what happens to us. There is a constant battle between good and evil, and good does not always win. Rose, God *can't* control all the bad things that happen, but God does what God can to make things better."

Mark's words struck at Rose's heart. The calm words that he delivered to her that evening, with such passion and commitment, changed her life forever. It forced her to really question the foundation of her faith. In the end, understanding dawned and Rosemarie felt reborn.

Mark and Rose continued to see each other regularly–for dinner, ice cream, or casual chats. Soon after Rose finished treatment, the Air Force transferred Mark to Texas. Shortly thereafter, Rose and Jim rediscovered their love for each other and were married. It was almost as if the Lord had kept Mark close at hand until he knew that Rose could make it on her own.

While many people touched Rose's life that year, Mark's touch was the most comforting of all. She had experienced a crisis of faith, and Mark had encouraged her to rediscover it at a time in her life when she needed it most.

. . .

Even though I walk through the darkest valley, I fear no evil; for you are with me; your rod and your staff–they comfort me.

—Psalm 23:4

Dear God, we understand that the forces of good and evil are present in our world. Sometimes it is easy to place the blame for our troubles at your feet. It takes courage to turn evil away and to look to you for our salvation. Please grant us the inner strength we need to turn our back on evil and to turn to you instead for our guidance and hope. Amen.

SEVENTEEN

Unmasking Cancer

✺

CAROLYN HAD NEVER FANCIED herself an artist. Truth be told, she actually couldn't create much of anything beyond stick people. So when she was presented with a unique opportunity to artistically create a mask that depicted her journey through cancer, she hesitated. Oh she was intrigued, all right, but she was a bit frightened, too. Her strength had always been found in her words, not in her art.

But after giving some serious thought to it, Carolyn decided to learn more about The Celebration Mask project before she decided one way or the other. The hospital she had received her treatment from–Froedtert Memorial Lutheran Hospital/Medical College of Wisconsin–had formed a partnership with the Milwaukee Art Museum. Together, they had a vision . . . to give their cancer patients and survivors an opportunity to artistically express their thoughts and feelings on the face of a mask. Each participant in the project was invited to have a plastic web mask made by the Radiation Oncology department. Traditionally, these masks were created for head and neck cancer patients to hold their head in position for pinpoint accuracy during radiation treatments. But this time, they were being used in a slightly less traditional way. Those who participated in this project were asked to decorate their masks to represent the journey's they took through cancer.

Carolyn was so struck by the importance of this project that she made the decision to participate. On her first evening she arrived at class a bit tentative. Because she had been unable to attend the first session, everyone in class was far ahead of her. Some of the masks looked positively spectacular. She was in awe and assumed (incorrectly) that the people who had chosen to participate in this project were all artists, or at the very least, individuals who thoroughly enjoyed creating with their hands. But as she began to talk to the cancer patients, she was struck by how similar they all were. They, too, had been hesitant about coming to class. Ultimately, their desire to share their journey with others overrode their anxiety. Their innermost hope was that they could offer a glimpse of what the cancer journey had been like so that others could feel some of the emotions and feelings they had experienced along the way.

As Carolyn sat with the untouched mask in front of her, she asked herself, "What is it that I remember *most* about cancer?" The first thing that popped into her mind was the extreme darkness she had felt, followed by brief hues of radiant color. Throughout her journey, she had come to experience the full spectrum of the rainbow . . . dark colors on downtrodden days, bright colors on pleasant days, and all the colors that fell in between on the days that fell somewhere in the middle. So Carolyn began to decorate her mask using color as her key theme. Inch by inch, her mask began to take shape. Oblivious to those around her, she painted, drew, and glued without a second thought to how others would perceive her mask. She found that it suddenly didn't matter anymore. This was a personal quest.

When Carolyn finished, she stepped back and looked at her creation. She realized that her completed mask was equally split into two parts. One showed the confusion and chaos that she associated with her diagnosis and treatment. The other depicted the peace and serenity she felt when her treatment was complete and she was cured. She recognized that the two halves represented before-and-after shots of her life with cancer. While she had not intentionally set out to do this, she was not surprised that she had ended there.

As part of the project, Carolyn had been asked to describe what her completed mask said about her cancer journey. She chose to express it in the following poem:

Churning emotions,
Spinning, spinning, always spinning.
Shock, fear, utter loneliness.
Patches of extreme darkness,
Punctuated by brief moments of graying hues and patchy sunlight.
Physical pain is dealt with, even welcomed,

It has a purpose—it is fighting the enemy.
Mental anguish is harder to suppress.
What I would give for one uninterrupted hour of cancer-free thoughts.
My family and friends rally at my side.
Their love is pervasive; their touch comforting.
But, even they cannot penetrate the loneliness,
Or the simple understanding that this is my battle, my battle alone.
A spiritual reawakening,
A sense that I am not really alone.
I don't have to fight this battle by myself.
I lift my concerns upward,
And He holds my hand and comforts me.
Time and time again.
As many times as I ask.
Then, I break through the darkness,
And emerge on the other side, cancer-free.
I am struck by the intriguing thought,
That being cancer-free will be like living a lifetime of springs.
The beginning of life anew.
Dazzling sunlight, comforting warmth, a sense of giddy joy,
That can't be suppressed.
I emerge reborn and embrace life.

Carolyn had initially thought that revisiting all the pain of her cancer experience would only serve to depress her. Instead, when she finished her mask, she felt cleansed. She realized she was proud of herself, not only with the creation of her mask, but also with her journey through cancer. She had tackled it head-on and had prevailed. She had revitalized her faith in the Lord, relying on Him fully. She had also experienced personal growth, making a better life for herself and her family. While Carolyn will never be thankful that she had cancer, she is very grateful that she went through this experience with her eyes wide open. Through God's grace, she has been reborn.

. . .

"In the same way, let your light shine before others, so that they may see your good works and give glory to your Father in heaven."

—Matthew 5:16

Dear God, enlightenment comes in many forms. Sometimes we are struck with clarity of thought with literally no effort on our parts. At other times, we search endlessly for the answers to our questions, with no understanding. We thank you for the opportunities that arise in our lives that help us discover inner peace and enlightenment. Please provide us with the courage we need to accept these challenges. Amen.

EIGHTEEN

Anything but Child's Play

❧

S HE WAS ONLY THREE. Only *three!* Her parents could not comprehend how it was possible that little Tracy had such a grown-up disease. They wondered how she could have a disease that had more letters in it than she was long. Rhabdomyosarcoma. That was the diagnosis. Dave and JoAnne couldn't believe what Dr. Martin was telling them. Their minds churned out endless questions. They couldn't understand why God would inflict such a deadly disease on such a young and seemingly perfect little girl. In their minds, cancer and little children just didn't seem to go together . . . not at all.

Cancer was not a novelty in little Tracy's family. Just two short years earlier, when she was only one, her mother had been diagnosed with uterine cancer. Dave and JoAnne had struggled through surgery and chemotherapy, all while tending to the needs of an energetic one-year-old. Throughout, they remained optimistic that JoAnne would one day live to see her daughter walk down the aisle . . . on her way to becoming a mom herself.

Now, just ten months after her chemotherapy had ended, JoAnne sat stupefied as the young doctor informed her and Dave that Tracy had a "very deadly form of cancer." They were told they had several choices:

1. Amputate Tracy's leg to stop the cancer's growth.

2. Undergo normal chemotherapy and radiation treatments, with an estimated survival rate of less than 40%.

3. Undertake extremely aggressive and massive chemotherapy and radiation treatments, complete with extended hospital stays, with the potential of 80% relapse-free survival, but an equally high potential of Tracy being killed by the treatment.

4. Do nothing and accept the consequences.

None of these options seemed particularly palatable in the eyes of Tracy's parents. But, ultimately, with the help of her doctor, they chose the most radical treatment plan, hoping that Tracy's body could tolerate the aggressive treatment protocol and that she would survive.

Tracy began her rigorous journey to a cure. The tumor was surgically removed, resulting in a ten-inch incision in her little leg . . . from thigh to knee. She was placed in a cast that covered nearly one-half of her body. The surgeon implanted a control line in Tracy to assist in the administration of chemotherapy. She began treatment immediately, alternating one week in the hospital with one week at home.

Tracy was a trouper throughout her treatment. She viewed the experience the way that only a child can. When she began to lose her hair, she exhibited the playful innocence of youth. Her mom and dad watched as their three-year-old daughter playfully grabbed handfuls of hair from her head, throwing it up in the air and giggling. They contemplated how totally different the ugly face of cancer can be from the vantage of a young child.

Tracy fought back with all the power she could muster. But over time, the steady drip of two powerful chemicals into her body took its toll on her white blood cells, causing Tracy to be ill more and more frequently. The number of days she spent in the hospital increased, with Tracy only being allowed to go home for one to two days at a time. Fevers ravaged her body, and infections fought to control her. Dave and JoAnne began to feel as if the third floor of the University of Chicago Hospital was their second home.

Through it all, Tracy fought with an outwardly endless reservoir of courage. She became a well-known patient on the floor, not only because of what she was going through but also because of her fighting spirit. Not always an easy patient, the nurses and doctors welcomed her temper tantrums and emotional outbursts, because they knew she would need this power and strength to get through all of her treatments.

Despite her illness, Tracy never lost her desire to engage in life and all of its goodness. Whenever Dad was at the hospital, she begged him to take her for walks so that she could experience all the sights, sounds, and smells of the hospital. Dave would lovingly put Tracy in a wheelchair, carefully juggle her IV lines, and walk her through the halls of the hospital, meeting and greeting everyone they met. The walks seemed to invigorate Tracy; Dave delighted in seeing the happiness creep onto her face whenever they met someone in the halls or experienced something new.

Spring marched on. Buds formed; flowers began to blossom; and birds returned from the South. As life emerged outside her hospital room, Tracy continued to work toward the rebirth of her own life. The dawn of spring also ushered in baseball season. Although it was hard to imagine, this little three-and-a-half-year-old girl was a huge Chicago Cubs fan. As she approached her fourth birthday, the nurses often asked Tracy what she wanted for her birthday. She continually told them she wanted a Cub cake as a present. Confused by her request, the nurses kept thinking she was asking for a cupcake. At long last, they understood what she was trying to tell them. "Well," the nurses thought, "If Tracy wants a Cub cake for her birthday, a Cub cake she will have!"

On the eve of her fourth birthday, after she had fallen fast asleep, the nurses snuck in and decorated Tracy's room. They strung red, white, and blue streamers from the ceiling and blew up Cubs balloons, hanging them all over her room. As sunlight broke, the nurses hugged and kissed Tracy and sang "Happy Birthday." They presented her with a special "Cub Cake" and her very own Chicago Cubs uniform. Tracy's fourth birthday brought incredible joy to both Tracy and her family. The nursing staff had made a profound difference in their lives.

Only days after Tracy turned four, her health took a turn for the worse. Her body was racked with infection, she spiked a fever, and sores began to cover her body. Despite strong antibiotics and loving and tender care from her family and her medical staff, Tracy's condition deteriorated rapidly. Dr. Martin examined her thoroughly and sought the advice of other professionals, but no one could determine the cause of her infection. Dave and JoAnne fervently prayed for their only child's life. Tracy's name was added to many prayer chains around the Chicago area. All had come to realize that her fate no longer rested in the hands of her physicians, but now would be determined by God.

Then unexpectedly, Dave and JoAnne were presented with an option. The University of Chicago had just been selected as one of two hospitals in the country to receive an experimental drug that might offer hope for Tracy. It was not approved by the FDA and had never been tested on humans, so it presented some very real risks. Dr. Martin explained that, through it offered hope, it might also cause long-term brain or heart damage. He went on to explain that it was so potent that it might kill Tracy. Although his words were certainly alarming, Dave and JoAnne recognized that the current course of action no longer represented a viable option. Without intervention of some form, they knew Tracy would not survive. So, knowing all the drug's inherent risks, they signed the release and asked Dr. Martin to proceed. As this new drug was injected into Tracy's little veins, Dave and JoAnne prayed that God would save their little girl.

Within less than an hour, Tracy's eyes began to clear and her fever inched downward. Soon she had regained enough strength to sit up in bed. She began to chat with her parents, who vigilantly sat at her bedside. Some of the spunk that Tracy was so well known for started to creep into her eyes. Tracy's speedy recovery was unprecedented–it was quite simply astounding. Dave and JoAnne wondered, "Was it merely coincidence that this drug became available at their hospital at the exact time in Tracy's life that it was needed most, or was it divine intervention?" Dave and JoAnne chose to believe in the miracle that had happened before their very eyes, recognizing that God had intervened in Tracy's life.

In the months and years ahead, the drug that had been used on Tracy quickly became the standard treatment protocol for children suffering from Rhabdomyosarcoma. Tracy had been a pioneer for a drug that would go on to save many, many young lives for years to come. God's great work continues.

As Tracy aged, doctors continued to monitor her health. Although there were occasional scares, the cancer never returned, nor did she experience the brain or heart damage that some thought may be a side effect from the experimental drug that had been administered to save her life.

One might surmise that one so young would easily forget her experience with cancer. But many memories remain implanted in Tracy's brain.

As Tracy's health improved and she regained energy, she became just like every other child. She couldn't wait to go outside, to run and jump, and to play with the kids in the neighborhood. Dave and JoAnne encouraged Tracy's behavior, believing she had a lot of life to catch up on. But too many parents looked at this bald little girl with sunken eyes and made the decision to cross the street to avoid her. Others forbade their children from playing with her, ignorantly assuming that their children might "catch" cancer from Tracy. Although Tracy felt like a normal child *inside*, her outward appearance falsely frightened many.

On Tracy's fifth birthday, just one year after receiving her Cub cake and uniform, she entered kindergarten. Like every other child that day, she was both nervous and excited. She had waited so long to go to a "big girl" school and was ready to meet all the new children there. Tracy had experienced so many non-childlike experiences in her short life that her parents welcomed the idea of her being "just another kid" at school. But after her very first day, Tracy came home and announced to her parents, "I'm not going back . . . ever." When questioned, her teachers agreed with Tracy's decision, telling Dave and JoAnne that she should be held back for one year. They explained, "Tracy has difficulty interacting." All these judgments were made after just one short day of school.

Dave and JoAnne turned to Dr. Martin, who had always provided them with the soundest of advice when it came to Tracy's welfare. He knew that Tracy's world had been turned upside down in the past few years. Not only had she dealt with surgery, chemotherapy, radiation, and illness, but Tracy's "Nana" had also unexpectedly died five months after Tracy's treatment ended. Nana was a very pivotal person in Tracy's life, and Tracy still felt a void where Nana had once been. During this time, Tracy's mother had also given birth to a new baby girl. Tracy's new sister, Lisa, had been diagnosed with some health problems of her own upon birth. She had two holes in her heart and had been forced to undergo open-heart surgery to repair the damage before reaching the age of one. With so many things in Tracy's life in a state of flux, Dr. Martin thought that, now more than ever, she needed a sense of continuity in her life. In his opinion, it was time for her to immerse herself in a normal environment and to interact with others her own age. He spoke with the school system and vehemently shared his viewpoints with them. They acquiesced, and Tracy stayed in school.

But that couldn't stop what the children would say and do to Tracy. Whenever Tracy wore shorts, the after effects of her illness were there for all to see. Her scarred and misshapen leg encouraged snide remarks and jeers from her classmates. Some children called her "Turtle" because she was weak and couldn't walk or run as quickly as they could. Others said her leg looked *funny* and laughed. To top things off, Tracy's body was so busy repairing the damage from the chemotherapy and radiation that she didn't grow at all for a few years, remaining quite petite.

Then, something happened in seventh grade that changed Tracy's life forever. One day in health class, her teacher began to talk about cancer. A classmate of Tracy's brazenly raised her hand and offered her opinion to the class, "I think it would be fun to get cancer. You'd get a lot of attention." This comment served as a rallying cry for Tracy. For the first time in her life, she began to speak out on the horrors of this deadly disease. She shared her experiences with her classmates, both publicly and privately, striving to help them understand how challenging and difficult cancer can be . . . especially when it affects a young child.

But despite Tracy's efforts, ignorance continued to rear its ugly head from time to time. When tracy was sixteen, a high school boyfriend made fun of her the first time he saw her in shorts and asked her to refrain from wearing them in the future. Instead, Tracy refrained from dating him again. She remembers family friends who publicly told everyone at a party not to eat the brownies Tracy's family had made because, "Two people in their family have had cancer, so there must be something wrong at their house."

But Tracy realizes that all of these experiences have made her a more decent person. She never teases or makes fun of anyone, because she understands that you never really know what is going on in that person's life. She doesn't take her health for granted and knows that good health can be snatched from you in a heartbeat. She believes in miracles and senses that God has a greater purpose for her on this earth. Today, she looks back and realizes that a life-threatening situation can make or break your life. She chose for it to make her life.

Tracy has also used cancer to help focus her life's ambitions. Now enrolled at Western Illinois University, she is majoring in journalism with plans to go to law school. Her dream is to represent the interests of cancer patients who have to deal with insurance companies that are not willing to pay for the care they so desperately need.

Tracy will always remember the loving touch of Dr. Martin. In high school when she struggled with algebra, he set aside an hour each night to tutor her over the telephone on her math assignments. When she got asked to junior prom, he offered the use of his car for Tracy to go to the formal in style. To Tracy's family, Dr. Martin is so much more than just a doctor and their daughter's hero; he is their treasured friend.

. . .

Let your father and mother be glad; let her who bore you rejoice.

—Proverbs 23:25

Dear God, we thank you for the doctors, nurses, and other medical professionals that are present in our lives. We praise you for the new drugs that scientists discover that help advance the cure rate of the deadly diseases that exist in our world today. With these actions, you prove to us that we should never give up hope and that our cure may be waiting just around the corner. God, we ask that you enlighten us with the knowledge we need to help, rather than hurt; to love, rather than tease; to welcome, rather than turn away. Amen .

NINETEEN

Running on Empty

❦

LORNA WAS FLYING HIGH. In a few days, she was going away for the weekend with her husband, Dennis . . . all alone. Her mother was coming to watch their six-year-old son, Carter, and their eighteen-month-old daughter, Jadef. With the care of her children in her mother's capable hands, Lorna had no reason to worry. She could go away for the weekend and thoroughly enjoy herself.

On top of the excitement of being alone with Dennis for one glorious weekend, Lorna was also looking forward to the purpose of their trip. They were attending a Christian marriage enrichment class, where she and Dennis would find new ways to continue to grow in their love for each other.

The road trip to their weekend getaway was quiet and peaceful, with Lorna and Dennis using each second of their precious time together to get caught up on all the things happening in their lives. As much as they loved being with their children, they really enjoyed talking to each other without *any* interruptions. Lorna and Dennis arrived at their hotel relaxed and excited. After meeting a few of the conference attendees, they snuck away to their room, anxious to prepare for the next day and to get a good night's rest.

Lorna awoke the next morning invigorated and recharged. She took a deep cleansing breath and inhaled the taste of freedom. Oh, what a weekend this would be! She could think of no better way to start the day than with a brisk run. She quietly pulled on her running clothes, laced up her shoes, and headed for the exercise room. Over the years, her daily run had become a treasured time, a time that was Lorna's and Lorna's alone, a time to reflect on all the things happening in her life, a time to work through her troubles, a time to thank God for his blessings. Somehow, her run always helped her gain a renewed sense of purpose for the day ahead.

After a few stretching exercises, Lorna headed to the treadmill. It wouldn't be as good as running outside, but she felt more comfortable in a gym than on the streets of an unfamiliar city. She started off slowly, easing into her run, working out the kinks she had acquired from sleeping on an unfamiliar bed. But just a few short minutes into her run, Lorna started to feel a little unsettled. Something wasn't quite right–she had stomach cramps. They weren't the kind of cramps you get from running too fast, being nervous, or eating the wrong kind of food. Something felt wrong *inside* her body. Lorna tried to break through the pain while running, hoping it would abate; but instead, it only intensified. Finally, she was forced to get off the treadmill. Shaking her head, with a bewildered look on her face, Lorna headed back to the room.

In spite of Lorna's strong desire to attend the marriage enrichment class with Dennis, she was frightened to be in a strange city, visiting a doctor other than her own. So with a heavy heart, she asked Dennis to take her home. He knew in an instant how frightened his wife must be to cancel their well-laid out plans at a moment's notice.

Lorna's symptoms continued to persist on the ride home. Both she and Dennis decided that the pain had escalated to the point that they needed to get to a doctor as soon as they arrived home. The initial tests conducted at the hospital indicated that Lorna's ovary was abnormally large. Based on the location of her pain, it was apparent that the enlarged ovary was most certainly the cause of the pain. Her doctor prescribed birth control pills, speculating that they would help to reduce the size of the ovary and make Lorna more comfortable.

The first few weeks following Lorna's visit to the doctor looked promising. The pain was definitely subsiding, almost to the point that Lorna didn't even notice it anymore. Without realizing it, she found herself beginning to slip back into the normal routine of her life with Dennis, Carter, and Jadef. Soon, the everyday demands of car pools, packed lunches, homework, and evening baths seemed to dominate Lorna's life once again. But just as she had begun to accept that her problems were behind her, Lorna was ripped out of a restful evening of sleep with a sharp, unending stab of pain. The pain was so intense that she found she had difficulty breathing. Lorna nudged Dennis awake, with a panicked look on her face, pleading with him to take her to the hospital.

The emergency room physicians conducted a quick, but thorough, physical examination of Lorna. They told Lorna and Dennis that they feared that Lorna might have ruptured something internally or that she had a twisted fallopian tube. Without hesitation, they insisted that she be rushed into surgery. There, the surgeon discovered an aggressive tumor that was already nine centimeters in size. The tumor had grown so rapidly that it had twisted Lorna's ovary, triggering severe pain. The surgeon, while surprised at his discovery, reassured Lorna that he was nearly certain the tumor was benign. According to standard protocol, he would send the biopsy to the pathology department when it opened the next morning, but he told Lorna not to worry. Lorna left the hospital relieved. She was no longer in pain, and the tumor was likely benign.

She gratefully sunk into bed that evening, settling into a disturbed and restless sleep. She awoke the next morning feeling groggy and uncomfortable. It was then that she noticed the pain in her chest. At first, she thought that the recent events in her life had opened her immune system to a chest cold. It made sense after all. But as the day wore on, Lorna found it increasingly difficult to breathe. Once again, a foreboding sense of gloom came over her. She began to sense that her *new* pain was somehow related to her *old* pain. In her mind, it only left one option—to take that now too-familiar trek back to the hospital.

Another visit to the ER led to a string of startling discoveries. Physicians discovered that Lorna's surgeon had accidentally ruptured her tumor and ovary as he removed them from her body. While not necessarily bad in and of itself, the second bit of news made this a profoundly disturbing issue. The tumor that the surgeon was so convinced had been benign had, in fact, been malignant. Lorna's entire body had been exposed to the cancer when the tumor ruptured. Doctors were now concerned that the cancer may have inadvertently been spread throughout her body. Thankfully, after further tests, doctors discovered that there was no sign of cancer anywhere in Lorna's body; it had not spread.

While analyzing fragments of the tumor, doctors began to piece together the sequence of events in her diagnosis. The tumor found in Lorna's body turned out to be highly sensitive to estrogen. When Lorna had taken prescription birth control pills, she had inadvertently fed the tumor's growth with a steady diet of estrogen. Ironically, the twisted ovary had saved her life. Without it, it was highly unlikely that the tumor would have been discovered in time to save her life.

Doctors thought the safest next step was to perform a complete hysterectomy. Lorna endured the rigors of the operation, recognizing that she had already been blessed with two beautiful children. She was not discouraged and felt it was appropriate that God bless other couples with children instead of her and Dennis. She then began a regimen of chemotherapy to insure that she would remain cancer-free far into the future.

Just six months after completing treatment, Lorna was back to running. But this time she was running a marathon to raise funds for the Leukemia and Lymphoma Society. As she crossed the finish line, Lorna triumphantly raised her arms over her head. Her excitement driven not only by the fact that she had just completed her first marathon but also by the realization that she had just completed the race of her life.

As Lorna looks back, she recognizes that God's hand was on her throughout her journey. She believes He wanted her to remain on earth for a while longer. There were just too many things that could have happened to take her life that year . . . a tumor that could have grown out of control, a rupture that could have rapidly spread cancer throughout her body, or a tumor that did not twist her ovary, providing no signal that something was wrong. Psalm 116 became a mantra for Lorna that year, rallying her to a physical, mental, and spiritual rebirth.

. . .

For you have delivered my soul from death, my eyes from tears, my feet from stumbling. I walk before the Lord in the land of the living. I kept my faith, even when I said, "I am greatly afflicted."

—Psalm 116:8–10

Dear God, at times, life appears to be a mystery. One day, we are feeling right with the world. We have people in our lives that we love and who love us. We are happy with what we do for a living and with what we have accomplished. Then one day everything is tilted on its side. Our life changes abruptly, leaving us feeling lost and defenseless. But soon we realize that we are not really lost. Throughout our journey, you are with us each step of the way. Thank you for being our constant companion through life. Amen.

TWENTY

The Angel Tree

MARINA WAS ON HER WAY to her mammogram . . . just like countless other times in her life. While she worried a bit each time, she had become accustomed to the routine. Each year she would drive to the clinic, register, change into a swanky hospital gown, have her mammograms taken, go back and sit in the waiting room, be told the scans were fine, get dressed, and go home. It was a ritual she had learned to take great comfort in.

This year, as Marina was going through her mammogram, her mind was on other things. She was juggling so many balls that rarely slowed down. As the technician did her job, Marina was thinking, "I hope this doesn't take too long. I have a number of errands to run today." Lickety split it was done, and Marina was asked to sit down and wait to make sure the films were fine.

A few minutes later, the technician came back and told Marina she needed to repeat the mammogram on her right breast. "No big deal," Marina thought. This had happened before. She probably had just moved and made the films blurry or something.

But when the technician returned a third time saying there was a small area in Marina's right breast they couldn't see and that they wanted to repeat the film again, Marina started to tremble. This was *not* part of the normal routine. But she submitted, and the films were repeated.

Then the technician came in and asked to do a *fourth* set of films. She told Marina that she needed to magnify that area of her breast so the doctor could get a closer look at it. By now, Marina was totally agitated. She nervously asked the technician, "What seems to be the problem?" The technician gave her the standard medical professional reply; "I am not at liberty to discuss this with you. Only the doctor can talk to you. I am just following his directions."

Without a moment's thought, Marina's eyes began to tear up. She asked to speak with the radiologist before completing the fourth set of scans. The doctor promptly entered the room, carrying two sets of mammograms–the one from the previous year and the film that had just been taken. Putting them side by side, he circled the same area on both mammograms. "See this?" he gently asked. "See *what*?" thought Marina. All she saw were gray and white blotches. To her untrained eye, the two mammograms looked exactly the same. She thought, "Excuse me, but *no*, I do not see that." But instead of voicing her frustrations out loud, she looked at the doctor with a dull questioning look on her face. The doctor made an attempt to reassure Marina, telling her it might just be a cyst, but in order to make a better diagnosis, he needed to magnify the area.

With his thorough explanation, Marina offered her complete cooperation. She continued to cooperate when her gynecologist asked to do an ultrasound of her breast and then later when he scheduled a core biopsy. Marina was told she would have the results of her biopsy within two days. While two days did not initially seem very long, oh, how the time dragged. Seconds felt like minutes, minutes like hours, hours like days. It was almost impossible to sleep for the two evenings prior to her appointment. Marina's mind never took a rest–it was constantly racing.

But finally, the day arrived. Marina, and her husband, Frank, made the now somewhat familiar trek to the doctor's office. They waited patiently one and a half hours past their scheduled appointment time for the doctor to appear. Exhausted from lack of sleep, Marina's head bobbed, and she began to nod off. Now, of all times, she found she could sleep! Go figure.

Finally, the doctor entered the room and announced that he had both good news and bad news. Before Marina could attempt to form an opinion on which she wanted to hear first, the doctor told them the tumor was malignant. Marina wondered, "What could possibly be the *good* news?" Dr. Branigan then told them that the good news was that the mass appeared to be quite small, suggesting that Marina would likely only have to undergo a lumpectomy and radiation treatment.

Marina struggled to accept the news. The tears slowly rolled down her cheeks as she began to absorb the true impact of his words. She wondered, "Could he have mixed the films up with someone else's? Was he sure it was *Marina* he was talking to? Do I really have breast cancer?" It didn't make sense. She felt totally fine. Heck, she couldn't even feel the lump in her breast. Marina thought, "Shouldn't I have *some* symptoms? Can someone so healthy actually have *cancer*?" The questions swirled around her brain.

Marina and Frank exited the room and trudged to their car, silent. They asked each other, "How can we possibly deal with this? How can we tell Liza, Ben, and Susan about this?" Shortly after arriving home, they gathered their children in their bedroom and shared the unsettling news with them. They explained that Mom would have to undergo surgery and radiation treatments but they had caught it early, so everything was going to be all right. They drew great comfort from their children.

As the days unfolded, Marina discovered that the mass was larger than initially estimated. It was located close to Marina's armpit, so unfortunately, there was also lymph node involvement. Marina squirmed as she realized that chemotherapy would now be added to her repertoire of medical treatment. So much for the good news.

Marina's path to recovery was a long one. She endured four chemotherapy treatments, followed by surgery, four more chemotherapy treatments, twenty-eight general radiation treatments, and five booster radiation treatments. Throughout her journey, Marina chronicled her experiences on her hospital's Web site, providing others with the opportunity to experience her joys, sorrows, nervousness, and despair. Total strangers began e-mailing Marina, offering words of encouragement and hope and promises to include Marina in their daily prayers. What had started out as a helpful project for the hospital had turned into a loving support network for Marina.

Marina took her role as reporter seriously, writing in her Internet journal often. She didn't hold back in her messages, but rather candidly exposed her physical, mental, and emotional turmoil to her readers. As Marina's journey became more difficult and she struggled to get through each day, her journal entries became more sporadic. That was when her readers and friends—led by the loving efforts of her sister-in-law—decided it was time to give the gift of hope to Marina. Her sister-in-law placed a Christmas tree on the front porch of Marina's house. She asked anyone who had benefited from knowing Marina, or from reading her journal entries, to add an angel ornament to the tree. With the tree placed outside

Marina's home, visitors would not have to disturb her. They could quietly hang an angel on the tree and leave just as quietly as they had arrived.

The original hope was that twenty to thirty angel ornaments would find a home on Marina's tree. But instead, nearly seventy-five angels fluttered on her tree. Many had come from complete strangers. Nearly all had very heartfelt messages attached to them. Each morning, clad in her robe, Marina would stand on the cold stoop of her house searching for the new angels that had arrived unannounced the previous evening. Marina was consoled, knowing that she had so many angels watching over her.

Looking back, Marina fully understands how much those angels provided daily respite from her suffering. Now each year, when she adds the angels to her Christmas tree, she fondly recalls all the people who made her life just a little brighter and a little more hopeful the year she had cancer.

. . .

How does God's love abide in anyone who has the world's goods and sees a brother or sister in need and yet refuses help? Little children, let us love, not in word or speech, but in truth and action.

—1 John 3:17–18

Dear God, our lives are so busy. In our rush to go on to the next task, we often become self-absorbed, focusing on ourselves. Please help us slow down the pace of our lives just a bit, so that we are aware of those around us who need help. So often, a few words, a friendly smile, an unexpected phone call, or an angel ornament can help lift the spirits of a friend or stranger. What might take so little effort and time on our part can make such a profound difference in the life of another. Amen.

TWENTY-ONE

The Chemo Cap Crew

❦

ELLEN ENJOYED A VERY SPECIAL RELATIONSHIP with her niece and god-daughter, Suzette. Their bond was so close that, to Ellen, it was very much like having her very own daughter. When Suzette married Mark, Ellen's warmth and love quickly spread to him. Later, the circle of love grew to include their children, Joshua and Emily Rose.

When Suzette was diagnosed with breast cancer, her family and friends quickly surrounded her with love and support. Doctors encouraged her to have a mastectomy in order to remove any doubt that all the cancer was gone. The surgery was successful, and Suzette was deemed cancer-free. Months of radiation and chemotherapy added another layer of assurance to her cure.

With Suzette's cancer gone, Ellen had time to think of other things. But somehow, her thoughts always drifted back to that fateful year when Suzette had suffered so greatly. Her cancer had deeply affected Ellen, to the point that she now yearned to do something to help put an end to this deadly disease. Ultimately, she chose to organize a group of employees at the company she worked for to participate in the "Making Strides against Breast Cancer Walk." Together, they encouraged as many friends and family members as possible to sponsor them in the walk. The first year was immensely successful, but Ellen was not one to be satisfied with the status quo. Her passion continued to grow and, like wildfire, spread to the hearts and minds of her coworkers, until they were 150 people strong. Today, Ellen's law firm is one of the flagship sponsors of the walk.

Then the devastating news came. Suzette's cancer had returned, and the prognosis was bleak. While doctors did not hold out much hope, Suzette did anything and everything she could to kill the cancer lurking in her body–surgery, radiation, and chemotherapy. She maintained a great attitude and built on the positive energy of those around her. She, and those who cared for her, prayed fervently for a complete recovery. But despite all these heroic efforts, Suzette's body surrendered to cancer at the age of thirty-nine, leaving her husband and two young children behind to remember her in spirit only.

While Ellen continued the annual five-mile breast cancer walk, she now desperately wanted to do something that could help cancer patients on a more personal level. Many of Ellen's waking thoughts were consumed with trying to devise a worthwhile project that would help breast cancer patients in need. And then, one day, Ellen was struck with a thought. During Suzette's years of chemotherapy, she had repeatedly lost her hair. She had tried wearing the turbans that so many other women had worn, but their polyester content made her head too hot. She also tried wearing wigs, but they were itchy and uncomfortable. In the interest of comfort, Suzette finally gave up on it all–no turbans, no baseball caps, no itchy wigs. Instead, she chose to go "au naturel."

It was this memory of Suzette that eventually pushed Ellen down an adventurous new path. She started thinking, "What if I could create a soft, comfortable hat that women could wear during radiation and chemotherapy?" After some careful planning, Ellen mobilized a team of women to help with this project. The Chemo Cap Crew was born. The first "production run" of hats, and every stitch sewn since, has all been made possible because of the generosity and love of private individuals.

Since the inception of Ellen's idea, over 1,000 chemo caps have been lovingly sewn and decorated by a group of thirty-two women. While the group primarily focuses on satisfying local needs, their hats have found their way all over the United States. The group has received countless letters from appreciative women who have thoroughly enjoyed their specially sewn caps. But all members of the Chemo Cap Crew agree that they have reaped as much or more from their labor of love as the patients have, as evidenced by their own words:

"Something happens when people sit down to sew chemo caps. A
rush of emotion brings forth a sharing or a healing as each person be-
gins to reflect upon her own cancer-related life experiences. One by
one, stories of loss and triumph, heartache and acceptance, surround

each cap, making it an even more meaningful experience for the volunteers. Even more touching is that the same feeling–the same wave of emotion–is experienced by the recipient."—Ellen

"As I get ready for work every morning, I look in the mirror and hope that I have a good hair day. But then I think about the women who lost their hair, due to chemotherapy or other circumstances, and I am thankful to have a hair day–be it good or bad. I know that making these caps will not help find a cure for cancer, and it won't change the lives of women living with cancer. But I hope that making these caps will help women smile, if not because the caps are fun and colorful, then because they know that these caps were made with love, faith, and hope."—Danette

"I pray that our caps are making a difference in someone's life. God bless those women, children, and men for what they all have to go through."—Tammy

"One of my best friends died after eight years of battling breast cancer. She always had a wonderful attitude, right up until she passed away. If this little bit helps to make people feel good about themselves during this 'not so grand time' in their lives, it's great, and it makes me feel good too."—Mary

"Life is best when you can give to others in a way that makes a difference in their life, whether it is just to bring a ray of sunshine and hope or comfort in times of sadness, trials, and loss."—Mary Jo

"I am thankful to do anything I can for anyone who has any need anywhere. This is just a small love gift to the ones who are hurting so much."—Mary

"I lost my sister to cancer just a couple of years ago. To watch this outgoing, vibrant woman age by leaps and bounds, right before my eyes, was heart-wrenching. I felt totally helpless. Sewing these hats is so easy compared to what cancer patients have to go through. I feel like it's the least I can do. It makes me feel good to know that I have provided a little joy in someone's pain-filled life."—Pamela

"It started off to be a challenge to sew just one button on a cap. But after I accomplished that, and the good feeling I felt when it was done, it made me feel complete knowing I was able to help someone out there. Now I can't get enough caps to sew!"—Victoria

"Rather than giving money and not knowing where it is spent, I make hats. I enjoy the cards and letters we receive from women who are enjoying the hats we make."—Gail

"It is one way I can make the corner of my world a little better. It makes me feel good that I am putting a smile on a face. I am hope-fully teaching my children how to give back to the world/community we live in. With all the wonderful things the chemo cap group is about, it does make me very sad that the need is so very great, that so many of our lives have to be touched and changed by cancer for-ever."—Ellen

The project that had started out as just a seed of an idea for Ellen has now blossomed into something far greater than she could ever have imag-ined. She has discovered that, unlike cancer, good deeds *can* be conta-gious. Ellen is thrilled with the success of her chemo cap program, but is saddened by the fact so many caps need to be sewn. Her hope is that one day soon a cure for cancer will be discovered, putting her out of business forever.

. . .

Be hospitable to one another without complaining. Like good stew-ards of the manifold grace of God, serve one another with whatever gift each of you has received.

—1 Peter 4:9–10

Dear God, sometimes it is so difficult to be a caregiver. As one single, soli-tary individual, we sometimes feel like we can't really make a difference.

Then we see someone who has indeed made a profound difference in the lives of others and we recognize that we may be able to do something after all. Please help us identify our own individual gifts and talents that we may put to work for others. Help our actions inspire others so that the chain of good deeds continues far beyond anything we could possibly imagine. Amen.

TWENTY-TWO

You Reap What You Sow

LORRAINE PACKED TO GO TO HER north woods cabin with joy in her heart. The cabin had been in Lorraine's family for over sixty-five years, and it had become a part of who she was. It was a quaint cabin situated in the densest of forests at the edge of a sparkling clear-water lake. Lorraine had many fond memories of all the family gatherings and joyful occasions she had experienced there. With the passing of her mother and father seventeen years earlier, the cabin had become Lorraine's, and she had no intention of ever giving it up.

Lorraine and her sweetie, Barney, were finally packed and ready to go. They had decided to take separate cars so that they would have more flexibility during the summer months. But, while they drove to the cabin in separate cars, Lorraine and Barney made the 300-mile trek driving next to each other the whole way. Barney had purchased two-way radios so they could stay connected, allowing them to talk incessantly on their journey. At times he sang sweet and melancholy love songs over the radio to Lorraine, causing her to grin like a young schoolgirl. Everything in her life seemed so perfect; retirement was turning out to be a pretty sweet deal.

The six-hour drive went rather quickly and before they knew it, Lorraine and Barney found themselves at the cabin. Lorraine sighed with a deep sense of elation. It always felt like coming home, no matter how long she had been away. As she gazed out over the lake, she felt the old familiar stirring within. "What a precious and beautiful sanctuary," she thought.

After settling in and unpacking, Lorraine began to pick up the pieces from where she had left them the previous summer. She called and visited old pals, renewing lifelong friendships. She particularly looked forward to the moments she would spend with her dear friend of many years, Fern. She couldn't wait to see Fern and give her a gigantic bear hug.

But Lorraine's visit to Fern was not what she had initially hoped for. Fern's health had been failing while Lorraine had been away for the winter. She had visited a number of doctors but none were able to tell her what was wrong. The latest doctor had speculated that she might have had a minor stroke at some point in her past, but he didn't appear to be particularly confident about his diagnosis.

Since Fern had never gotten a driver's license, Lorraine became her chauffeur that summer. She was determined to help Fern discover the true cause of all her ailments so that she could start to feel better again. Together they visited doctor after doctor, trying to find one that could help improve Fern's quality of life. Their travels finally led them to a neurologist who properly diagnosed Fern's condition. She was told she had ALS–Lou Gehrig's disease. Fern and Lorraine were shocked to discover that there was no cure for this dreaded disease.

Together they drove home in companionable silence, each trying to absorb the news in her own private way. Finally Fern broke the silence by asking, "When are you going home, Lorraine?" Lorraine explained, "One of my favorite authors is going to be at the public library on October 5th. We'll probably be leaving for home the day after that." Fern looked at Lorraine sadly and commented, "Then I'll have to die before then." Lorraine encouraged Fern to think of the life she had yet to live. She desperately tried to inspire hope in her dear friend, but found that her words fell on deaf ears. It appeared that Fern was determined to die and to do it before Lorraine left for the winter.

Each day Lorraine faithfully drove the twelve miles to Fern's apartment with bags of groceries and prepared foods that she thought Fern might be able to eat. Sometimes they'd sit for hours, reminiscing over the good times they'd shared. At other times Fern was sad and Lorraine would read stories to her or sit by her side as they watched her favorite movies, hoping to cheer her up. Lorraine always kept a positive attitude around Fern, encouraging her with stories of hope and love.

While Lorraine carved out time in each day for Fern, she also spent many relaxing and entertaining hours with Bernie. They enjoyed each other's company so much. It didn't matter if they talked, played games, sat by the lake, or went antiquing in nearby towns together. As the summer days faded into evenings, the hours up north seemed to melt away.

As is typical of life as a senior citizen, Lorraine had aches and pains that came and went. She never thought twice about these pains; they were just a part of her everyday life. But by mid-summer, she noticed a constant and nagging pain in her right leg. She visited a chiropractor, which provided temporary relief from the pain, but somehow it always resurfaced. While Lorraine thought it a bit odd, she chalked it up to sciatic nerve problems. Since Lorraine's income and medical payments were solely driven by what she received from Social Security and Medicare, she never overreacted when it came to visiting doctors. She always wanted to be able to support herself financially, so there was no use in running up unnecessary doctor bills just to be told she had arthritis or sciatica. Lorraine continued her daily visits to Fern, determined to see her through her time of crisis, while giving little thought to her own ailments. But the next two months saw a continued degradation in Lorraine's health. She found that she could no longer walk without a cane. At night the pain was almost unbearable. In order to get into bed, she would have to use her arms to drag her legs together and up into bed.

At the same time, Fern's condition had continued to worsen. She had great difficulty swallowing and had become extremely weak from her lack of proper nutrition. Finally the day dawned on which Fern was out of options. Barney drove Fern and Lorraine to a local hospital, finally placing Fern into the able-bodied hands of the doctors and nurses.

Throughout the month of September, Barney and Lorraine regularly visited Fern. Lorraine's leg had become so weak that Barney would get a wheelchair upon entering the hospital and would wheel her to Fern's room. Lorraine remained strong, placing the needs of her dear friend before her own. She never let Fern see the amount of pain she, herself, was in. Each day she sat at Fern's bedside, holding her hand and offering her comfort. On September 28 Fern gave up her fight and peacefully passed away in her sleep. Her funeral was held on October 6, the exact day that Lorraine had told her friend she would be leaving for home. Four months earlier Fern had told Lorraine, "I'll have to die before then." It appeared that she had delivered on that promise.

With no more planned trips to care for Fern, Lorraine and Barney prepared for their journey home. Each approached the day with mixed feelings. They were sad to leave the cabin and all the memories of Fern behind, but were looking forward to getting home before the cold winter months descended upon them. But they also approached the day with a bit of anxiety. They had driven up north in separate cars, so each would need to make the trek back home separately. Both understood that this journey would be challenging. Lorraine would have to use her arms to pull on the leg of her overalls in order to get her foot on the brake or accelerator. Having the strength to depress either was highly doubtful. There would be no time for fast reflexes; that was for sure. Every move would have to be premeditated, *well* in advance. While Lorraine was frightened beyond belief, she questioned what alternative she had. She knew there was no one else available to drive her car home and she certainly didn't want to leave it by the lake all winter long. She and Barney couldn't stay at the cabin any longer, because the cabin was not winterized; it was only intended to be a summer home. No matter which way she looked at it, they had to brave the drive home and hope for the best.

The day to leave the north woods dawned bright and sunny. The cabin was cleaned, the suitcases were packed, and both cars were loaded up. Lorraine was at her bathroom sink, sprucing up as she prepared to leave. Her hand was propped on the ledge of the bathroom sink, holding the majority of her weight, when it slipped. Her body followed the motion of her hand, and she rapidly fell to the ground. Instantly, Lorraine's body was racked with blinding pain. She struggled to catch her breath and to gain control of the situation, but it was impossible. The pain was so excruciating that all she could do was lay on the bathroom floor sobbing.

Barney quickly called 9-1-1, and the rescue squad hurriedly made its way to the cabin. Finding a way to get Lorraine onto a backboard, with as little pain as possible, proved to be a monumental task. But that pain was nothing compared with what lie ahead. Twenty miles of bumps, turns, and curves caused agonizing pain. Finally the ambulance arrived at the local hospital–the same hospital in which Lorraine had visited Fern just a few short days before. But the tables were now turned. This time, the patient was Lorraine, and it was Barney who was holding her hand and reassuring her that everything would be all right.

Lorraine was told she had a broken hip. Unfortunately, because of the size of the small, country hospital, there were no orthopedic surgeons on staff. So it was necessary to transfer Lorraine to a hospital thirty-five miles away. A heavy dose of pain medication and two compassionate ambulance drivers helped ease her pain as much as possible on the way to the second hospital.

The grace of God shone its beautiful face on Lorraine that day. Because of rapid improvements in medical science, a hip surgery that just five years earlier would not have even been attempted, was now a reality. The surgeon told Lorraine that he would operate and make her hip like new. Lorraine went off to surgery, with a sigh of relief. While she knew the recovery and physical therapy would be tough, she was more than ready to do whatever was necessary to get the use of her leg back and to get some relief from her chronic and debilitating pain. As the anesthetic pumped into Lorraine's veins, she faded off, buoyed by hopeful thoughts for the days ahead.

As Lorraine slipped through the darkness and her head began to clear, she realized that the surgery was already over. She instantly noticed a hospital chaplain sitting by her side. The chaplain offered her a tender smile and asked the question that would turn Lorraine's world upside down in a matter of a few short seconds, "Lorraine, what are your thoughts about cancer?" Lorraine learned that a tumor the size of a baseball had been slowly eating away at her hipbone all summer long. Although this news of a cancerous tumor was certainly disturbing, Lorraine's pain was completely gone. She felt better physically than she had in a long, long time.

Lorraine was once again transferred to a larger hospital–this time to one in a medium-sized community that offered a cancer center. Her first appointment with her oncologist was less than encouraging. He speculated that Lorraine's hip was likely not the primary site of her cancer and told Lorraine that it had probably metastasized from another part of her body. As he looked at Lorraine, he bluntly said, "Your whole body is probably full of cancer." With her pain gone, Lorraine's feistiness had returned. Before she could stop the words from spilling from her mouth, she sputtered, "Well, that is *your* opinion. I guess I'll have a few more tests and opinions before I press the panic button."

But the glum conversation with her doctor had taken its toll on Lorraine. She left, feeling sad and discouraged. As the Medicab pulled up her daughter's driveway, Lorraine was surprised to see that her son-in-law, Dan, and her grandson, Rob, had been busy at work since her last visit.

They had built a wheelchair ramp. At first, Lorraine wondered, "Now, why did they build a wheelchair ramp? Who is going to use that?" Then the truth broke through the cloudiness of her brain, and she realized that the ramp had been built for *her*. The reality of it all finally weaseled its way into the cracks and crevices of Lorraine's brain: she was sick, she had cancer.

The days and nights ahead were nothing short of ghoulish. Lorraine could only lie in bed for three-hour intervals before she became tremendously sore and uncomfortable. Then her daughter, Christine, would get her up and sit her in a chair, propping her legs up on pillows that were balanced on a footstool. She worked directly with the physical therapist to learn what she could do to ease her mother's pain and massaged Lorraine's leg, providing as much relief for her mother as possible. Christine did this night after night, day after day, without a single complaint. She, Dan, and Rob had kindly and generously welcomed Lorraine into their home, accepting all the responsibilities without a single disparaging word.

As she recovered, Lorraine waited for confirmation from Medicare that they would pay for the tests that would help to verify or refute the presence of more cancer in her body. The wait was interminable. The carefree days spent at the lake with Barney seemed so very long ago. Lorraine had learned to replace those days with the new routines in her life–bed to chair to wheelchair to bed, punctuated by visits to her doctor and physical therapist.

Finally word came back from Lorraine's HMO that a CAT scan had been approved. The hospital chose to scan Lorraine's entire body, fairly confident that the tumor in her leg was not the primary site of her cancer. Unfortunately, the test confirmed their suspicions. Lorraine had a tumor on her left kidney. As the doctor prepped Lorraine for yet another surgery, Christine came to the hospital with a book that Lorraine's hometown pastor had sent her, "There's No Place Like Hope." This gift was provided at a time when Lorraine desperately needed a sense of hope and promise. It reassured Lorraine, helping her to realize that her life rested in God's hands and no one else's. She clung to the words in that book with every ounce of her fiber and being. There was no way she was going to accept a diagnosis of death, not when she had so much to live for.

The kidney surgery went smoothly and was declared a success. The tumor was encapsulated and had not spread. To be on the safe side, the oncologist suggested that Lorraine undergo radiation therapy. Finally, one month later, Lorraine was released from her doctor's care and allowed to make the long overdue trip back home. Barney came to live with Lorraine for awhile, to help ease her back into her life and to be her companion and friend . . . just as Lorraine had done so unselfishly for Fern just six months before. At times Lorraine wondered what she had ever done to deserve so much love, first from her daughter and her family, and then from Barney. But then she smiled and thought, "I guess you reap what you sow."

. . .

Bear one another's burdens, and in this way you will fulfill the law of Christ. . . .So let us not grow weary in doing what is right, for we will reap at harvest time, if we do not give up. So then, whenever we have an opportunity, let us work for the good of all, and especially for those of the family of faith.

—Galatians 6:2, 9–10

Dear God, every once in awhile, a person comes along in our life that reminds us of the true power of love. They give of themselves, their talents, and their love without a second thought. Often they put the needs of others before their own. God, help these people to inspire us to action. Help us to give of ourselves rather than constantly taking from others. Amen.

TWENTY-THREE

On the Wings of an Angel

EDWARD WAS AN EXCEPTIONAL thirteen-year-old. He radiated pure sunshine from every inch of his very being. He always seemed to be surrounded by many people. People liked to be by Edward because they drew energy and strength from him.

Edward came from a large family. He had seven siblings; he fell somewhere in the middle. His family had always been very close, cheering each other on at Little League games, applauding at dance recitals, and grinning with pride whenever someone in their family had something wonderful happen. When one of their brothers or sisters was ill, the whole family pitched in, helping with chores and offering words of encouragement. When one was sad, the others worked hard to coax a smile from his or her lips.

While their family was equally supportive of one another, Edward was the crown jewel, and everyone knew it. From toddler on, it was apparent that he was special. He didn't make fun of other children, didn't tease his brothers and sisters, and didn't judge others. In his mind, God had made all the children of the world and He was the only one who could judge their worth.

When Edward was diagnosed with leukemia, he seemed to take it all in stride. He didn't complain, despite the need for painful bone marrow biopsies and brutal chemotherapy treatments. It often seemed as if *he* was the one cheering up the other members of his family, rather than the other way around.

Edward's diagnosis was grim, for he had a very deadly form of leukemia. Doctors speculated that he only had six to twelve months to live. But Edward and his family were determined to beat the odds. The first year came and went, and Edward was not only alive, but in remission. His profound faith in Christ, the strong support from his family members, and his engagingly positive attitude had helped Edward live beyond all previous expectations. But doctors cautioned Edward that it was highly likely that he would relapse. They explained that while the leukemia could go into remission numerous times, each relapse would prove to be far more difficult to overcome than the last. As time marched on, Edward relapsed twice; in each case, he successfully forced the cancer back into remission.

Before anyone realized it, the day of Edward's high school graduation dawned. It represented one of the happiest and proudest moments in his family's life. They had never, in their wildest dreams, anticipated that this day would come to fruition in Edward's life. On graduation day Edward's only goal was to be like every other eighteen-year-old sitting in the audience that day. Just like them, he had plans for his life too. He wanted to pursue a career and recognized that he first needed to earn a college degree. So Edward enrolled in a nearby college and joined all the other freshmen that year, full of hope and wonder.

Throughout his first two years of college, Edward made many new friends and expanded his horizons. While he studied hard, he enjoyed every moment of his campus life. As he began his third year of college, Edward started to feel increasingly more tired with each waking day. Deep inside, he knew that the leukemia had returned, but he wasn't ready to admit it to himself . . . much less to his family. The last battle had been so difficult that he wasn't sure he'd be able to survive the rigorous treatments once again.

Edward finally came to grips with what was going on inside his body and visited his oncologist. A subsequent bone marrow biopsy confirmed his suspicions. Not only was the leukemia back, but it was back with a vengeance. There was a sinking feeling within the hearts of everyone in Edward's family that *this* time the cancer was here to stay.

All his life, Edward had enjoyed art and had hoped that one day he would have the opportunity to visit the Louvre in France. He yearned to see the paintings created by Leonardo da Vinci, Raphaël, and Jan Goassert. After hearing the disturbing news, Edward asked his parents if there was any possible way he could make this trip. Edward's family was determined to honor his request, especially because he had never asked anything of anyone ever before. Together, his family and church helped to raise the funds needed to send Edward, his father, and a priest from their church to France.

Edward was ecstatic as they set off on their trip. While at times he was weak during their travels, he savored every moment he spent in the museum, marveling over the great works created by the loving hands of the artists on display. He came home filled with the sights, sounds, tastes, and smells of France. His buoyant spirits encouraged his family, but Edward's health continued to deteriorate. Shortly thereafter, he was readmitted to the hospital. With a look of supreme peace on his face, he slipped into a coma. The doctors spoke with Edward's family and informed them that it was highly unlikely that he would ever reawaken. They estimated that within the next few days, Edward's life would be over, leaving them with only his spirit and the memories of his wonderful existence. Edward's family was beside themselves with pain and sadness.

His mother in particular was filled with immense grief. She had spent most of Edward's life holding him close and loving him, somehow understanding that his time on earth would be too short. In her grief, she fervently prayed to God, asking, "God, watch over and protect my son." She worried constantly that Edward would be alone and frightened without her by his side.

With so many siblings, Edward was rarely alone in his hospital room. His brothers and sisters took turns reading him stories and telling him about their days. All had a sliver of hope that he might be able to hear them and would be reassured by their stories.

On one particularly rare day, Edward's mother, Mary, found herself alone by his side. She held his hand and reassured him, while at the same time experiencing fear about what awaited Edward. As she sat there, she prayed constantly, working each bead of her rosary numerous times. As she finished her rosary, she prayed using her own words, "Lord, show me that Edward is going to be all right. *Please show me.*" All of a sudden, Edward's eyes fluttered. At first, Mary thought her eyes were deceiving her. She wanted so desperately for Edward to awaken that she thought she had created an illusion in her mind. But then his eyes opened wide and clear and settled on his mother. He squeezed his mother's hand and asked, "Isn't she beautiful, Mom?" Mary looked around the room, expecting to see a nurse who had soundlessly entered Edward's room, but instead she found she was alone with her son. "Who?" Mary asked. He replied, "The angel, Mom. She is *so* beautiful." Then Edward quietly sank back into a coma with a peaceful look on his face.

Edward passed away a few hours later. As Mary shared her experience with his father, brothers, and sisters, all knew that God had sent her the sign she had prayed for. God did not want Edward's family to worry about him, but instead wanted them to know that he had found safety and tranquility in God's kingdom.

. . .

I am going to send an angel in front of you, to guard you on the way and to bring you to the place that I have prepared. Be attentive to him and listen to his voice; do not rebel against him.

—Exodus 23:20–21a

Dear God, death is rarely welcome. We struggle when we lose those who are close to us, especially when they leave us prematurely. But somehow it seems as if you blessed these young people from the very day they were born. They exhibit an amazing capacity to love with little to no effort. It is almost as if you put a full life's blessing into those short years they spent with us on earth. Thank you for that gift and for the angels you send to show us how astounding eternal life will be for those who believe in your goodness. Amen.

TWENTY-FOUR

The Kind Stranger

❧

JILL CASUALLY WALKED INTO THE BOOKSTORE. As she strolled through its aisles, she tried to get her bearings, thinking, "Now, just where would the journal section be?" After wandering aimlessly for a short time, she stumbled upon it, pleased to see that it extended for an entire row. "Surely," Jill thought, "I'll be able to find a journal that fits my needs."

She started on one end, picking up journals and flipping through pages. Jill had been told that it really didn't matter what kind of book you journaled in. It could be as simple as a blank sheet of paper or a spiral notebook. She knew the key was to select a journal that would allow her to openly express her feelings in the most comfortable way possible. Jill decided that she wanted a journal that provided a source of daily inspiration, something that would force her to think positively about what was happening in her life.

While Jill had originally been pleased that the bookstore had so many options, it suddenly felt overwhelming. Before she knew it, her concentration wavered and she was lost deep in thought. She found herself wondering how she was going to cope with what life had dished out. At the moment, life felt a bit too large for her to handle. Jill pulled back from her thoughts and started to amble through the rest of the store in search of . . . *something*. She just wasn't sure what that something was.

As she stood in front of another section of the store, staring blankly into space, Jill was approached by a stranger. The kind-looking woman had a book in her hand. She looked Jill in the eye and said, "I saw you looking at journals and noticed you walked away empty-handed. Might this journal interest you?" Jill took the journal that was in the stranger's hand and opened it. On the top of each page was an inspirational Scripture verse. Jill thought to herself, "This is exactly what I was looking for."

She asked the woman who had just handed her the journal, "How did you know?" A faint smile crossed the stranger's face as she answered, "You looked so grief-stricken. I thought this journal might help." Before she could stop herself, Jill quietly muttered, "I have cancer. I was just diagnosed a few days ago." She went on to explain that she had been looking for an inspirational journal that would help guide her through the difficult journey she knew lie ahead. The young lady looked at Jill and asked, "What is your first name? I would like to include you in my daily prayers." "Jill," she said. The well-intentioned stranger stood up, squeezed Jill's shoulder, and told her everything would be all right because God was by her side.

Jill never saw that woman again. She never even found out what her first name was. But a five-minute conversation with this kind stranger totally changed her outlook on her illness. She purchased that journal and immediately began to write her thoughts and feelings down. The very first words that graced the pages of her journal were dedicated to the earth angel that God had sent down to help Jill through her struggles.

. . .

"Then the king will say to those at his right hand, 'Come, you that are blessed by my Father, inherit the kingdom prepared for you from the foundation of the world; for I was hungry and you gave me food, I was thirsty and you gave me something to drink, I was a stranger and you welcomed me. I was naked and you gave me clothing, I was sick and you took care of me, I was in prison and you visited me. . . . Truly I tell you, just as you did it to one of the least of these who are members of my family, you did it to me.'"

—Matthew 25:34–36, 40b

Dear God, how is it that you always seem to know just when we need a special friend in our lives? At our most desperate hour, you send us a gift of love, friendship, and support . . . a gift that helps us travel the difficult waters so much more easily. We thank you for all the coincidences that occur in our life, which are not really coincidences after all, but instead divine intervention. Amen.

TWENTY-FIVE

The Path of Discovery

NANCY WAS MENTORING a young woman through confirmation class at her church. Julie was a remarkable young lady, and Nancy had grown quite fond of her. At the same time, Nancy had found that she, herself, was growing spiritually as she coached Julie through the book of Luke and other relevant passages in the Bible.

On one particular Saturday, the confirmation class and their mentors traveled to Calvary Presbyterian Church to learn more about the roots of Christianity and to walk through their labyrinth. Nancy, in particular, was really looking forward to this experience. She had heard stories about how enlightening and liberating the labyrinth had been for previous confirmands and their mentors and was curious if she would find answers to some of her questions there.

Nancy had been a cancer survivor for nearly two years. For all the pain and suffering that she had endured that fateful year she had cancer, there was one thing she was absolutely certain about—she had never before, or since, felt that intimately close to God. Looking back, she realized that the closeness she felt that year had been so very calming and comforting as she had struggled through cancer. Now, years later, she wanted that closeness back, but just couldn't seem to rekindle the fire with quite the same intensity. Nancy was hoping that her spiritual walk through the labyrinth would be the answer to her prayers to become closer to God.

Prior to being involved with the confirmation class, Nancy had never heard of a labyrinth. While she had been told what it was, she found herself going to the Internet to do a little searching on what to expect. During her search, she learned that labyrinths have been around for centuries. They had originally been designed as a path of prayer to help monks get in touch with the inner soul. But, in recent years, people from all walks of life were striding through labyrinths, using them to promote self-reflection and to encourage a closer relationship with God.

When Nancy and the confirmation class arrived, Justin greeted them at the door, explaining that he would be their guide for the day. He took them to the sanctuary of the church, pointing out that Calvary's labyrinth sits inside a Celtic cross. Justin explained that the labyrinth was designed to take each participant on a journey to be closer to God or Christ and that there was no one right way to go through it. With a chuckle, he said, "You can walk it, crawl it, or skip it. It is totally up to you."

And so, Nancy began her journey. It was difficult at first because there were so many distractions. Everyone was all bunched together almost walking on each other's heels. Nancy could feel their breath on the nape of her neck and had a hard time focusing. She tried to relax and to empty her mind of all thought, but she struggled. So instead, she began to concentrate totally on the path itself, its straight aways and its slight turns, first to the right, then to the left. Soon she calmed down, and random thoughts began to enter her mind.

When Nancy reached the center of the cross, she sat cross-legged on the floor and let her thoughts consume her. Ironically, while just minutes ago she had been aware of every person, sight, and sound in the church, she now heard nothing but her own thoughts. She saw nothing but the sunlight reflected through the stained-glass windows, forming intriguing colored mosaic patterns on the floor. After sitting for some time, Nancy began to feel reenergized and redirected. She felt as if she had a new purpose in life and finally had clarity on how she fit into God's plan. She began to realize that she couldn't start her new life until she reached the end of the labyrinth. She stood up hastily, driven to reach the end of the labyrinth as quickly as possible. As she finished, she felt instantly compelled to put her thoughts in writing.

> "I was so struck by how the labyrinth is like life. Sometimes we have many twists and turns in our lives. Some of these turns represent good times, others demandingly difficult. We can choose to learn and grow from each. Then there are the straight aways, the periods in our life when all is well. Life floats along effortlessly, with no interruptions and no bumps. But just when we start to relax and enjoy these times, bang,

there's another turn . . . and then another . . . and then another. Sometimes, the turns come so rapidly, we can't catch our breath—like the year I had cancer. But even then, I knew there would be straight paved roads when the journey wouldn't be as difficult. I knew my future was secure."

Nancy found this experience, quite simply, amazing. She had entered the labyrinth hoping for a spiritual reawakening, an opportunity to get as close to God as she had the year she had cancer. But instead, she came to realize that the year she had cancer was a special and unique year. For during that year, Nancy had desperately needed to be intimately close to God in order to cope with the fears, anxieties, and disillusionment of her diagnosis. God had answered her call and had carried her through most of her journey. But now, Nancy's life was not encumbered with all of those challenges. It began to dawn on her that while God would always be an integral part of her life, it was time that she relied on her own internal strength to move forward with her life, trusting that He would always be there for her in times of need.

. . .

Trust in the Lord with all your heart, and do not rely on your own insight. In all your ways acknowledge him, and he will make straight your paths. . . . It will be a healing for your flesh and refreshment for your body.

—Proverbs 3:5–6, 8

Dear God, we recognize that being faithful can be easy at times and that, at other times, it can be extremely difficult. We know that just as the ocean ebbs and flows, so does our understanding and interpretation of your Word. Please grant us the vision to find our way through all of life's tribulations. Be by our side when our life is not going well, to hold our hand and to ease us through our journey. Amen.

TWENTY-SIX

Sweet 16

❧

NEW YEAR'S EVE HAD BEEN A BLAST! What sixteen-year-old girl who had an evening of fun and laughter with her dearest high school friends, wouldn't have a great time on New Year's Eve? So what if she had a little trouble breathing and there was a little pain in her chest? Judy rationalized that she had probably just overdone it a bit.

But as she awoke on the first day of the New Year, Judy knew something wasn't quite right. It was getting more and more difficult to breathe, and the pain in her chest was not subsiding. She figured it was time to tell her mom and dad. After telling them, they in turn decided it was sensible to seek medical attention. A lot of bugs were going around; maybe Judy had contracted something serious like pneumonia . . . something that necessitated the care of a physician.

After thoroughly checking Judy over, the doctor agreed it was unusual for someone of her age to be experiencing this combination of serious symptoms. He decided to order chest x-rays and asked Judy and her parents to wait for the results, concerned that there might be a problem.

Ironically, the doctor in charge of Judy's care was a long-time personal friend of the family. While this was comforting for Judy and her parents, Dr. Vukovich was faced with an extremely difficult situation. He had to be the bearer of the alarming news that the chest x-ray had revealed a tumor the size of a grapefruit on Judy's left lung. Judy's lung also appeared to be filling up with fluid, which was likely contributing to her pain and difficulty in breathing. The small-town hospital in Kokomo, Indiana, was equipped to drain the fluid in her lung and give her medication to ease the pain, but they needed to transfer Judy to Methodist Hospital in Indianapolis so that she could tap into the resources of a larger, better-equipped hospital.

Judy struggled to comprehend what was going on. This just didn't happen to seemingly healthy sixteen-year-olds. She thought, "You don't go out to celebrate New Year's Eve with your best friends one night and end up in the hospital the next day with news like this." As the day progressed, Judy had an uncanny premonition of what was to come. She was overpowered by the sense that she had cancer. In fact, she was nearly sure of it. The fact that their family friend was not only willing but *adamant* that he reassign Judy's care to another physician at a larger hospital confirmed the seriousness of her condition.

Judy was whisked off to Indianapolis, where surgeons awaited her arrival. Before she could comprehend what was happening, she was prepped for biopsy surgery and sedated. Following surgery, Judy and her parents waited one interminably long twenty-four-hour period for the results of the biopsy and then received the shocking diagnosis. Judy had mesothelioma—a rare form of lung cancer caused by exposure to asbestos. Doctors conceded that there was no plausible explanation for her diagnosis. She had never smoked a cigarette in her life. No one in her family had ever worked in the mines. Her father owned a jewelry store, with no asbestos in sight. It was perplexing. Yet here she was, being told that she only had a 10% chance of surviving lung surgery, much less any of the radical treatments her body would be exposed to if she were fortunate enough to live through the surgery. Her odds of surviving five years after treatment were set at less than 5%. Judy wondered if her 16 years on earth would be coming to a close soon. She repeatedly found herself asking God, "Why?"

Judy's journey began with surgery. Unfortunately, the first surgery proved unsuccessful. The tumor rested between her lung and the periocardiomembrane of her heart and it was much too large to remove. Instead, Judy would have to rely upon chemotherapy to hopefully shrink her tumor so that her doctors could surgically remove it later.

And so the treatments began—every three weeks for six months. The drugs were so strong that Judy often threw up for hours on end after each treatment. She required blood transfusions to give her the strength she desperately needed to weather the chemo storm. Blood counts and Oncovin™ shots were also weekly rituals. Judy struggled day after endless day, praying for the strength to outlast the cycle of treatments.

Then Judy's tumor showed signs of shrinking. The medical staff was stunned by the extraordinary developments in her health. They had never had much confidence in the treatments they were subjecting Judy's body to . . . in their minds it represented a "last-ditch" effort. Wisely, they had chosen to not share this view with Judy and her family. Judy was responding to the chemotherapy in a way unlike anyone had ever seen in the past. She and her team of doctors were rewriting medical history

With this latest turn in events, Judy's medical team wanted to provide her the best possible odds of surviving the next surgery. After conferring, they opted to send her to Sloan-Kettering Memorial Hospital in New York City for what they hoped would be history-making surgery. So Judy and her parents headed off to the Big Apple . . . the home of Times Square, the Statue of Liberty, Carnegie Hall, and Broadway. But unfortunately, Judy wasn't going to New York to have the time of her life; she was going there to fight for her life.

Judy instantly fell in love with the entire staff at Sloan-Kettering. They were so warm and encouraging that she immediately trusted them. When they suggested that Judy's left lung be removed in an effort to increase the probability of her relapse-free survival, Judy and her parents immediately agreed. The doctors were careful not to delude Judy; her odds of long-term survival remained exceedingly low.

The staff pampered Judy in every imaginable way as the day of surgery approached. But the best gift they could have given to a sixteen-year-old girl who had been denied all the culinary pleasures of frequenting her favorite fast-food joint was to allow her to order *anything* and *everything* she wanted to eat. Their lively and positive attitudes buoyed her spirits and put her in as good a mood as possible prior to embarking on the most difficult journey of her life.

To return the infinite love they had shown her, on the morning of her surgery Judy took out a tube of lipstick and drew a large red heart on her chest. Inside the heart, she left a special message for her surgeons, "Good luck! Love, Judy." Her message warmed the hearts of her surgeons as they diligently worked to remove the cancer from her body. Their hard work and determination paid off. They successfully removed Judy's left lung, carefully checking to make sure the cancer had not spread, and closed her chest with a feeling of a job well done. Judy was cancer-free. She had surpassed yet another seemingly unconquerable hurdle. Judy was a living miracle.

Following surgery, Judy was up and about rather quickly, regaining her strength and starting to push forward with her life. But doctors remained concerned. Her cancer was so viciously aggressive that they wanted to be sure that no microscopic cancer cells were left behind to cause problems for Judy in the future. So to be on the safe side, they scheduled her for six more months of potent chemotherapy treatments.

Judy hung tough through all her treatments, determined to emerge triumphant. Just as in her previous chemotherapy sessions, there were days that proved to be endless, days on which she felt so incredibly ill that she wondered if she had survived the surgery only to be taken down by the treatment. But in the end, she won the battle. Sloan-Kettering elatedly told Judy that she was cancer-free.

As Judy muses on the story that played out in her life nearly thirty years ago, she recognizes that she is a truly unique individual. She is the longest and oldest living survivor of mesothelioma in the country. She remains in communication with the doctor who started her on this miraculous journey. He is now eighty-six years old and welcomes every phone call and letter he receives from Judy, for she represents the greatest success story of his medical career.

Judy continues to see doctors for an annual checkup. Her approach to life is greatly changed since that fateful New Year's Day so many years ago. She recognizes that life can turn on a dime, just when it appears that it is so full of hope and promise. She recognizes the power of prayer and the strength of a positive attitude. She, more than just about anyone, recognizes that miracles do happen and that it is possible to survive cancer, no matter what the odds.

. . .

"For truly I tell you, if you have faith the size of a mustard seed, you will say to this mountain, 'Move from here to there,' and it will move; and nothing will be impossible for you."

—Matthew 17:20b–21

Dear God, so often poor statistics and discouraging words lead us to lose hope. We are told to expect the worse, so we do, forgetting that with you, all things are possible. We ask that you silently encourage us, especially in the direst of circumstances, so that we never lose hope. Please inspire others to pray without failing for the impossible to happen. Amen.

TWENTY-SEVEN

The Sign

WHEW, ANOTHER DAY DONE. Thank God," Maureen voiced to herself. She had managed to put in an eight-hour day at work, shuffle one son back and forth to baseball and another to piano lessons, all while entertaining her three-year-old with animal crackers in the backseat of her car.

Maureen decided it was finally time to grab a little time for herself . . . to pamper herself just a bit. She filled her bathtub up to the top with hot water and sudsy bubbles and dimmed the lights so that only a hint of light cast shadows around the room. As she sunk into the tub, she exhaled a deep, gratifying sigh. Ah, the water felt deliciously warm and soothing. She closed her eyes and breathed in the aromas around her. Maureen totally gave into a sense of relaxation, enjoying the peaceful solitude of her safe haven.

Once she had unwound, Maureen started performing a breast self-exam. She had found that it was the best place to do her exams because she could take her time and do a really thorough job. Over the years, she had become quite familiar with the irregularities she occasionally found, so she tried to do the exams around the same time each month, eliminating as many monthly abnormalities as possible.

As Maureen was finishing up her left breast, she felt something slightly different than usual. There was a little lump where there hadn't been one last month. It was so small she almost missed it; even knowing it was there, it was hard to find. Maureen knew it was possible to get calcifications from time to time and wondered if that's what she had found. It nagged at her mind for a few days before she decided to call her gynecologist to request an appointment.

After examining her breast, Maureen's doctor agreed that she should undergo further testing. To her relief, the tests were clean, showing no evidence of any abnormal growth in her breast. But Maureen's doctor did not share her relief. Instead, he told Maureen, "I don't like the feel of this, even though the pictures are clean. I'd like to do a needle biopsy." The results of the biopsy came back, and Dr. Traylor's worst fears were realized. Maureen had cancer. Subsequent tests revealed that eight of the sixteen lymph nodes that were removed from her body also tested positive for cancer. Maureen's cancer had been inside the wall of her chest, virtually hidden from the scans. This diagnosis turned Maureen's world upside down. Yesterday, her life had been filled with baseball games, piano lessons, and family outings. Today, her priorities had been totally rearranged through no fault of her own.

Maureen prepared to take on the toughest year of her life. She endured the pain and the recovery of her mastectomy, keeping a positive attitude throughout. Her only goal was to conquer the cancer and get on with her life. Chemotherapy began, and she learned to deal with the side effects. She fought back the nausea and the exhaustion and counted the months, weeks, and days until all of her treatments would be completed. But counting days proved frustrating; there were just too many to count. The more Maureen endured, the more down and depressed she became. She began to feel that the odds were stacked against her and that there was little hope of survival.

During her next appointment, Maureen told Dr. Traylor that she was becoming overwhelmed with the fight and feeling totally worn out. She went on to explain that she was having great difficulty sleeping. Feeling tired all the time only seemed to fuel her dark thoughts. Maureen so desperately wanted Dr. Traylor to tell her she would be fine and that she would emerge from this battle as a cancer survivor. In a desperate attempt to bribe him, she told him she would give him NSync tickets for his daughter, if he would just tell her she would be cured. Of course, she knew it was all a pipe dream and that there were no guarantees. She knew there wasn't a doctor in the country that would willingly give her one. But, oh, how she wanted one. As Maureen prepared to leave the room, Dr. Traylor came back in and asked, "Maureen, you're Catholic, aren't you?" Maureen replied, "Yes." As he reached into his pocket, he told her, "I have something just for you," and handed her a prayer card of St. Peregrine, patron saint of cancer patients. As he left the room, she mumbled, "Thank you."

Maureen trudged to her car. She opened the door and sank into the driver's seat, mentally and physically drained. The tears began, slowly at first, and then fell in a constant, unrelenting stream down her face. All she could think was that her doctor, instead of telling her she was going to live, had told her, "All that's left for you is prayer." As she sat there and absorbed the full impact of the news, a sob caught in her throat. She picked up the card and looked at it. The picture on the front was blurred through her tears, but Maureen turned the card over and began to read the words printed there. To her astonishment, St. Peregrine's feast day was May 2–her birthday! She immediately picked up her cell phone and called Dr. Traylor. "Doctor, did you know that my birthday is the same day as St. Peregrine's feast day?" she asked. His answer was spontaneous and heartfelt, "Yes! Why do you think I gave you that card? I think you have a connection with this saint."

And so Maureen prayed to St. Peregrine . . . again and again and again. Amazingly, her life seemed to improve. The darkness lifted, and the sun began to peek through the clouds. And then understanding dawned. Maureen knew she was going to be just fine. She knew that her faith would help heal her.

Ironically, although Maureen has found several St. Peregrine's cards since that special day, all of them show his feast day as May 1 *not* May 2. She has come to realize that the *one* card that Dr. Traylor gave her had specifically been meant for her. It was a sign that she was going to be all right.

. . .

Then Jesus said to him, "Unless you see signs and wonders you will not believe."

—John 4:48

Dear God, sometimes we are like Thomas. We doubt your presence or the wonder of your works. It can be so difficult to believe when we cannot see you, hear you, or touch you. It seems that our doubt is greatest when we struggle the most. God, please help us understand that sometimes you speak to us on a very personal level by offering us a sign. Open our eyes so that we can see these special signs. Help these wonders escalate our faith in you. Amen.

TWENTY-EIGHT

Best Friends

THEY HAD BEEN BEST FRIENDS FOR twenty-five years. In those years, they had never held back anything from each other, always sharing their innermost hopes, fears, and dreams. They had been through the best of times: the births of their twins, job promotions, building a new home, and celebrating birthdays, anniversaries, and other milestones. They had also been through the worst of times: the near-death of their son, a lost job, and the deaths of grandparents and parents. They always knew they would be there for each other; there was never a doubt in their minds.

When Leja was struck with cancer, Chad was by her side. He was her rock in every imaginable way. He cooked and cleaned. He drove the children to their after-school activities. He boosted her up when her spirits were low and rejoiced in her triumphs with her. Leja had beaten cancer, and her family had rejoiced. They settled in to start a new chapter in their lives.

But cancer had changed Leja in so many ways. She was not the person she had once been. Physically, she had a number of annoyances that were with her each day–some little, some not so little. None were life threatening, to be sure. But just the same, they were a constant reminder that she was a survivor.

Leja had also changed emotionally. Other cancer survivors understood, but it was hard to explain the emotional turmoil to someone who had never had to personally deal with cancer. The cancer permeated her thoughts nearly every day. Once in awhile she'd get a reprieve, but something always happened to bring it right back to the forefront. Every time a new friend, coworker, or church member was diagnosed with cancer, she felt their pain. Every time a cancer organization asked for her money, time, or talents, she gave with open arms, hoping to advance the cure rate of cancer. She never wanted anyone to have to suffer through this experience, so she always tried to find a way to help.

She had changed spiritually, too. She would never understand how someone who did not have strong faith could weather the cancer storm without God's divine grace and love. She had become firmer in her faith and often looked to God for guidance and support.

In short, Leja was no longer the woman whom Chad had married. She had felt the changes happening in their marriage over the last few years. But in the past five to six months, they were more pronounced than ever. He never seemed to listen to anything she said anymore. He interrupted her when she was trying to share something important with him and then never asked her to finish what she was saying. He made inappropriate comments about her in front of their friends and children—something he had never, ever done before.

She, in turn, had started to mimic his behaviors in an attempt to lash back at him, hoping he would feel her pain and change his behavior. In time, she started to pull away and began to keep more things inside. She began doing more things without him and often escaped to the romantic lives of the fictional characters in the books she read. But she felt empty. Even her closest girlfriend couldn't seem to fill the hole that Chad had started to carve out in her heart.

She began to be sad more often, and the children noticed. Leja shrugged it off and explained that her body was busy repairing itself, leaving her with less energy and enthusiasm for life. She told them not to worry, because everything was fine. In truth, she wasn't sure if her healing body was contributing to her sadness or not. But she was sure that her relationship with Chad was having a profound effect on her attitude.

One evening as they lay in bed, Chad asked, "How are we doing?" She wasn't really surprised by the question. Of course he had also noticed that their relationship had changed. You would have to be blind not to see it. The conversation started out innocent enough. Both rationalized why things were different in their marriage. They were exceptionally busy at work. The children and their activities were taking up much of their spare time. Their life was planned with so many events that there was just no time to relax. The truth was that many of these things had occurred before in their marriage, often simultaneously. While they might have struggled for a short period of time in the past, Leja and Chad had always found their center of balance, and life had once again proceeded smoothly. But this time things just seemed different.

As the conversation continued, Chad finally told Leja what he felt was at the core of their troubles. He felt she was talking about cancer too often. He went on to explain that this was one time that their personality differences were not working in their favor. Leja was an extrovert and a kindhearted "Dear Abby" of sorts. She helped others get through their troubles by helping them talk through their feelings. She offered a helping hand whenever and wherever needed. Chad, on the other hand, leaned toward being somewhat of an introvert. He preferred to deal decisively with a problem and then to store it away in a safe little compartment of his brain.

At the end of the conversation, he said, "I feel like such a jerk. I'm sorry." Leja reassured Chad, "It's okay. It's good to be open and honest with your feelings." But then she came to realize that he was apologizing to her *before* he delivered the crowning blow. After a few stutter starts, Chad finally said what he had intended. He asked Leja to stop sharing this part of her life with him. He explained that he was on overload. He needed to stop thinking about cancer so much, and the only way to do that was to have her keep her thoughts to herself. He ended the conversation by saying, "I love you." Leja just could not find it in her heart to repeat the sentiment. She rolled over on her side, with her back to him, and said good night.

As her mind churned and the warm, salty tears fell on her pillow she recalled the Scripture verse they had chosen for their wedding vows from 1 Corinthians, chapter 13, verses 4 to 7. "Love is patient; love is kind; love is not envious or boastful or arrogant or rude. It does not insist on its own way; it is not irritable or resentful; it does not rejoice in wrongdoing, but rejoices in the truth. It bears all things, believes all things, hopes all things, endures all things." Fifteen years earlier, Chad had taken Leja's hand and proudly repeated the words "for better or for worse." She thought, "This is part of the 'worse,' and now he is abandoning me so that *he* can feel better."

Leja was hurt beyond measure. She acknowledged to herself, "Yes, I am a changed woman. Cancer has left its permanent mark on my very heart and soul." She understood that there were times when she still worried about a new and unexpected pain, an upcoming scan, or insurance claims that didn't seem to get paid. She wondered, "How can he ask me to remain silent over all of these things?" This man who lay next to her in bed had been her best friend for countless years. How could he ask her to shut down a major part of who she was? Leja had heard of cancer survivors going through these same marital problems when the battle was over. Maybe it wasn't so much the difference between her and Chad. Maybe, instead, it was the difference between men and women. Women dealt with their problems by talking through them and commiserating with other women. Men, on the other hand, dealt with their problems by burying them far inside their psyches.

Leja tossed and turned, turned and tossed. She wondered, "Is it absolutely necessary that I shut down a major part of who I have become? Will I now be forced to bury my feelings in an attempt to save our marriage?" It just didn't seem fair. She was the one who had persevered through the painful journey brought on by cancer. Now she was being asked to endure yet another difficult transformation.

The questions swirled through her mind, "Just how far did this request go? If I am invited to a reception that is somehow related to cancer, should I invite him or not? If a friend of mine is diagnosed with cancer, should I keep that inside too? If doctors find a spot on one of my scans, should I bravely shoulder the fear and pain on my own?" She wondered what was left if this was what he was asking of her. It didn't matter from which angle Leja looked at it—their marriage had taken a decidedly major turn in the wrong direction. Both she and Chad had different opinions on the subject, and it appeared that neither would change their outlook. Leja was at a loss over what to do.

She lay in bed for as long as she could and then silently got up and went downstairs. She sat quietly in the family room, staring into the shadowy darkness, feeling totally spent. She asked herself repeatedly, "How can I handle this rejection?" Then it came to her. God was always there for her. God would never abandon her, no matter how bad life got. God would be there through thick and thin. God was the best friend that would always be by her side. Without a solution in mind, she prayed to God and asked for help and guidance.

She also remembered: "It is human to err, divine to forgive." How many times had she spoken those words herself? Would she now be a hypocrite if she chose to not live by the very words that she had asked others to live by? Christ himself had said to forgive not one time or seven times, but seventy-seven times. Leja knew that she had always enjoyed a strong relationship with Chad. It was unfair not to give this solid tree with deep roots the opportunity to grow a new branch that reached in a slightly different direction. It would take hard work and effort on both of their parts, but Leja knew there was plenty of love left inside both of them to make it happen. Leja prayed that after both she and Chad had time to think about it they would find a place where they could meet in the middle, a place where both could be happy and where they could begin to develop a new relationship as best friends.

The next evening when Leja returned home from work, a big bouquet of flowers was waiting on the counter for her. With nary a word, Leja felt the immediate and measurable change in Chad. He listened attentively as she spoke. He offered encouraging words. He held her tight throughout the night as they slept. As if by magic, their friendship once again blossomed. Each had taken a few steps towards each other and had found a meeting place somewhere in the middle. Leja then realized that God had answered her prayers, helping each of them rekindle the seeds of their love and friendship.

. . .

Put away from you all bitterness and wrath and anger and wrangling and slander, together with all malice, and be kind to one another, tenderhearted, forgiving one another, as God in Christ has forgiven you.
—Ephesians 4:31–32

Dear God, the path we travel is not always an easy one. We encounter bumps and potholes in the road of life. Sometimes the hill that reaches in front of us seems endless. We falter and wonder for a moment if we are courageous enough to make it to the top. But then we find the strength we need deep within us and start our journey. When we reach the top, we are amazed at the magnificent view; it is breathtaking. All of a sudden, the journey seems worth every ounce of effort we put into it. God, thank you for granting us the courage and tenacity we need to climb the hills in our lives. Thank you, also, for the glorious view from the top. Amen.

TWENTY-NINE

Three's the Charm

KATHLEEN PATIENTLY FOUGHT HER way through the congestion on the interstate as she slowly inched her way into work. While she disliked her daily journey to the university, she loved her job, making the trek worth the added stress she encountered each day. As Kathleen plunged headfirst into her work, she realized it was going to be another busy day. But that was fine with Kathleen. She often found that being busy made the day fly by so much more quickly.

As the day progressed, Kathleen started to feel ill. She thought to herself, "Darn!" She had been doing such a good job of not catching that flu that was going around the university. Now it looked like she wouldn't be able to avoid it any longer. Finally, Kathleen found she did not have the strength to focus on her job and informed her supervisor that she was heading home for the day. The ride home was exhausting. Kathleen tried to fully concentrate on the road and the traffic, despite her pain and discomfort. When she finally drove into her garage, she felt as if she had just completed a marathon. Kathleen headed straight for her bedroom, stripping off her clothes along the way. She searched her drawers for the most comfortable pajamas she owned. Just before sinking into bed, she popped two aspirin into her mouth and then snuggled deep under the warmth of her comforter. Kathleen figured that after a day or two of rest, she would be as good as new.

But as she lay in bed, her symptoms seemed to intensify. The abdominal pain appeared to be far worse than the kind of cramps she usually got from the flu. Sitting up helped, but she was so tired that all she really wanted to do was lie down. Finally, Kathleen situated herself in the recliner in her living room and sank into an agitated and pain-filled night of sleep, hoping she would feel better the next morning. But she didn't. After spending the better part of the next day feeling quite dreadful, Kathleen's husband chose to drive her to the urgent care clinic, somewhat against her wishes. She was still trying to convince herself that this was just a nasty flu. He, on the other hand, thought it might be more serious.

By the time Kathleen arrived at the clinic, the pain had intensified to a new level. Even Kathleen now agreed that it might be something more serious. The doctor in the clinic performed a thorough physical examination. He poked and prodded Kathy's stomach, inducing a number of uncontrollable coughing fits. After repeated bouts of violent coughing, Kathleen began to cough up blood. This downturn in Kathy's health met with an immediate reaction from the doctors. They quickly placed Kathleen on a gurney and hurried her into the open doors of an ambulance. They did not want to waste any time–they wanted her in a hospital. Kathleen began to shake violently. The implications and seriousness of the situation were descending upon her in a big way.

The emergency room was bright, loud, scary, and impersonal. It seemed as if a long line of doctors and nurses each took their turn poking and prodding Kathleen's stomach. Through it all, Kathleen continued to cough up blood and to be battered by extreme abdominal pain. Eventually, a doctor decided it was best to intubate her, placing a tube down her throat in an effort to eliminate some of the excess blood.

Kathleen was taken into an examination room to have a CT. The acute pain in her stomach, the discomfort caused by the tube, and the horror of what was happening caused Kathleen to feel the fuzzy edges of a panic attack. She fought for control, trying desperately to remain in touch with her feelings. As she floated in and out of consciousness, an ER nurse sat by her side, holding her hand. She was the earth angel whom Kathleen had prayed for. She helped to reduce Kathleen's fears and allowed her to gain some sense of control over her emotions.

Several radiologists quickly read the CT results, sharing their observations with Kathleen and her husband. There was a large, unidentified mass in her stomach. The doctors didn't know where the tumor had emanated from. They didn't know if it was malignant or benign. But they did know that it was exceptionally large and that it was not supposed to be there. It most definitely needed to come out. The doctors immediately called in an OB/GYN to perform the surgery.

After waiting for some time, Dr. Wiedmann self-assuredly strode into Kathleen's hospital room. "Hi, I'm Dr. Wiedmann," he uttered as he grasped Kathleen's hands in his own. He seemed to exude self-confidence from every pore of his body. Kathleen immediately felt relieved, placing her life in the hands of this seemingly competent surgeon. Dr. Wiedmann reviewed all of Kathleen's test results, as well as her vital signs. He quickly concurred that she needed surgery and needed it quickly. He talked to Kathleen gently, explaining all the details of what she would be going through. For the first time that evening, Kathleen felt that someone was talking to her like she was a real person.

Kathleen was whisked into the operating room and into the able-bodied hands of Dr. Wiedmann. She fell into a deep, drug-induced sleep and awoke later to feel the tightness of a blood pressure cuff on her arm. Kathleen asked the nurse "Is the surgery over already?" "Yes," the nurse replied, "but you'll have to wait until the doctor comes in tomorrow morning to explain everything to you." The idea of waiting did not sound very encouraging, but before Kathleen could think to object, she had drifted off to sleep again, heavily sedated with pain medication.

Thankfully, the remainder of the night was uneventful, and the doctor arrived before Kathleen awoke. As her eyes fluttered open, Dr. Wiedmann came into focus. She immediately read the lines of concern written all over his face. He explained that he had found a fifty-pound tumor connected to her left ovary and a second, baseball-sized tumor connected to her right ovary. He had been forced to perform a complete hysterectomy. In the process, he had also removed some of the lymph nodes in the immediate area. The pathology department was checking both the tumor and the lymph nodes for evidence of cancer.

Kathleen was stunned. Just two days ago, she was living a normal life. All of a sudden, she was over sixty pounds lighter and could quite possibly be fighting for her life. The doctor had told her that he had been so astounded by the shape and size of the tumor that he had his staff take pictures of him holding it. Kathleen looked at the pictures and was shocked—it looked as if Dr. Wiedmann were holding a large watermelon in his two hands. It was truly difficult to comprehend that that *thing* had been in her body just yesterday.

When the biopsy results came in, Kathleen and her husband were told that the tumor had indeed been cancerous. She had ovarian cancer. Fortunately, the lymph nodes had tested benign; the cancer had not spread beyond the primary site of the tumor. Kathleen was now a cancer survivor.

This experience was, most certainly, a life-changing event for Kathleen. As soon as she recovered, Kathleen and her husband began volunteering for the American Cancer Society and The Fantasy House for Cancer. She managed to get her life back in order . . . and then some. Kathleen was one hundred pounds lighter as a result of the removal of the two tumors, her altered diet, and her improved lifestyle. She was learning to listen to her body, paying close attention to all of its nuances.

Time sped by, and Kathleen reached her four-year anniversary of being cancer-free. It was such a terrific feeling. While still visiting her doctor every six months, she had become more and more optimistic with each visit. On this particular day, Kathleen approached her doctor's office with a smile on her face. She was feeling good and she knew she looked great. Dr. Wiedmann, too, was pleased with how well Kathleen seemed to be doing. He completed the physical exam and scheduled a routine CAT scan for Kathleen.

When Kathleen hadn't heard from Dr. Wiedmann for several days after her CT, she called. With a comical, foreign accent, she asked, "So, tell me doctor, am I going to live?" She chuckled a bit. There was a pregnant pause that extended a bit longer than comfortable. Then Dr. Wiedmann replied, "Kathleen, I found a very small mass in your abdomen during your physical. The CT scan confirmed my suspicions. I am sorry, Kathleen, but you will need more surgery." He went on to explain that the medical staff was perplexed. They couldn't understand how a tumor could be there when all her female organs had been removed. Kathleen was totally deflated. Just when she had started to forget her entire cancer experience, this had to happen.

Kathleen's operation was scheduled for one week later. The week dragged by slowly as Kathleen worried that the growth would once again test positive for cancer. The day of surgery finally arrived. This time, Kathleen found she was hyper aware of everything happening around her. She sensed each and every sight, sound, smell, and physical sensation in the operating room. While she had been through this once before, it all felt like the first time because she had been in such excruciating pain four years ago that she had been totally oblivious to her surroundings. The tears began to trickle down her face as the reality of what was happening lodged itself in Kathleen's brain. Thankfully, the anesthesia did its job, and she fell fast asleep. When she awoke, the doctor had great news. He was successfully able to remove the entire tumor. Subsequent biopsy results were also the best possible case scenario—*benign!*

Kathleen recovered quickly from her surgery and launched herself whole-heartedly into a new project. When she was a small child, her grand-mother had taught her to crochet. Kathleen now put that skill to work, crocheting robes and gowns. She checked around town and found an organization that would gladly accept her donations for cancer patients and survivors. In Kathleen's mind, it was perfect. Her robes and gowns offered the promise of comfort and warmth for others who were experiencing the same traumatic diagnosis she had earlier in her life.

Before she knew it, another four years had passed. Kathleen continued to be vigilant about scheduling regular doctor appointments and CT scans. While she generally felt quite healthy, from time to time she experienced minor twangs of pain on her right side. When she explained the pain to Dr. Wiedmann, he suspected it might be the result of adhesions caused by her two previous surgeries. Repeated scans continued to come back clean, helping to ease any worry that Kathleen might have had. But as time wore on, Kathleen's pain intensified, making her increasingly uncomfortable. Despite encouraging test results, both Kathleen and her doctor were concerned that something just wasn't right. Ultimately, Dr. Wiedmann made the decision to do an exploratory laparoscopy to see if something was going on that could not be detected on the scans.

Kathleen showed up at the hospital at the scheduled time, with surprisingly less fear than the previous two times. Before she knew it, she was once again awake and talking to Dr. Wiedmann. He had spent two hours removing a multitude of little bumps all over her intestines. Cancer was once again ruled out, to the relief of all. Strangely, Kathleen was diagnosed with endosalpingiosis. This ailment was usually found on the female organs of women during pregnancy. Without female organs, it had attached itself to Kathleen's intestines.

Today, two years have lapsed since Kathleen's third surgery. She is thankful that her health ailments have, in many ways, reversed her life for the better. She eats better, lives a healthier lifestyle, and has lost over one hundred pounds. She appreciates each day that God has given her. She works for several cancer organizations, helping to raise funds to eliminate this deadly disease, and her afghans have found their way into the homes of many cancer patients who have welcomed her loving touch. Kathleen believes that her life is indeed blessed.

If the four-year cycle of surgeries decides to repeat itself a third time, Kathleen realizes she will have to deal with that problem when it happens. In the meantime, she chooses to not worry, but instead, to focus on all the good that life has to offer.

. . .

He alone is my rock and my salvation, my fortress; I shall not be shaken. On God rests my deliverance and my honor; my mighty rock, my refuge is in God. Trust in him at all times, O people; pour out your heart before him; God is a refuge for us.

—Psalm 62:6–8

Dear God, sometimes we take the good life we lead for granted. We live one day at a time, doing what we normally do, without taking time to smell the roses along the way. Then something happens that stops us dead in our tracks, and our life changes in an instant. We struggle to cope with the adversity that we are facing. But then we turn to you and understand that you are always there for us. Amen.

THIRTY

The Sword and the Shield

BREAST CANCER? It can't be possible." Mary Jill was floored by the diagnosis. Not only was it cancer, but the cancer had spread to her lymph nodes and it was one of the most deadly and aggressive forms of breast cancer. She felt alone, frightened, and overwhelmed. She questioned God, "Am I going to die? What did I do to make myself so sick? Am I a bad person? Is that why I got this?" Mary Jill's first thought was that God had abandoned her; in fact, she began to wonder if God even existed. For the first time in her life, her faith was on shaky ground. Nevertheless, she prayed because it was what she had done all her life. It was what she knew. In her prayers, she asked God for comfort, a sense of hope, and a strengthening of her faith.

No sooner had Mary Jill questioned God and his existence when letters, phone calls, flowers, and well-intentioned visitors arrived at her doorstep. Countless other people told Mary Jill they were praying for her. She was overwhelmed with all the goodness that was present in her life, especially at a time when she needed it most.

Mary Jill underwent a mastectomy and spent several days convalescing in the hospital. She awoke one day to feel her feet being soothingly massaged. "Oh, that feels delightful," she thought. As she opened her eyes, she saw her husband, Rich, kneeling by her bedside, deep in prayer. She looked kindly at him and said, "Thanks for massaging my feet, Rich. It feels *so* good." Rich lifted his tear-stained face and looked at Mary Jill with a perplexed expression on his face, saying, "I didn't massage your feet, honey." Mary Jill tenderly lifted her head to gaze down at her feet and saw a soft muted light glowing around her feet. At that very moment, she felt a strong spiritual presence in her hospital room and realized that God had armed her with a sword and shield to battle her cancer. She was not alone. A few days later, Mary Jill headed home from the hospital. As she departed, she realized that her spirituality had greatly intensified in the last five days. She now felt more equipped to tackle her cancer physically, mentally, and spiritually.

As the chemotherapy dragged on, Mary Jill felt more and more vulnerable. She was tired, so tired that little tasks such as taking a shower or fixing lunch for her daughters seemed impossibly difficult. She vomited at all hours of the day, draining the reservoir of strength she had tucked away for the times when she would need it most. She experienced pain everywhere, especially in her arm. The pain there had intensified to the point that Mary Jill didn't have the strength to use it at all. She anxiously asked Rich, "What is wrong with me? This can't be normal." Rich kept reassuring her, "Don't worry, you'll get better." Mary Jill's oncologist echoed what her husband had told her. She thought Mary Jill was tolerating treatments quite well. But deep down inside, Mary Jill knew something very wrong was happening inside her body. Ten days into her descending health condition, Mary Jill collapsed in the bathroom of her home, vomiting blood. Rich rushed her to the emergency room, extremely concerned with his wife's worsening condition.

Doctors discovered that Mary Jill had a very serious internal infection. For four to five days, they tried to drain it, while at the same time barraging her with potent antibiotics and much-needed blood transfusions. Nothing seemed to work. The doctors were concerned that if they couldn't get her infection under control, they might lose her. The chemotherapy had taken such a toll on Mary Jill's body that her immune system was too weak to fight the infection. She was in so much pain that she pleaded with God, "Either let me go or let me get well. I'm too sick to continue this battle." She faded in and out of consciousness. At one time, she felt her bed rocking back and forth in an uncontrolled sort of frenzy. The room appeared to be artificially lit as she spun around in circles. Her IV flew around with her, at one time to her side, then at the foot of her bed. Just when she was certain she could no longer tolerate this unforeseen roller-coaster ride, everything suddenly stopped. Mary Jill felt ensconced in a comfortably warm blanket of soft light. She felt secure and safe and was no longer afraid. At once, she knew that God was at her side. Miraculously, Mary Jill fought her way through the infection, as well as the subsequent chemotherapy and radiation treatments. Once she had visualized God as her sword and shield, she fully understood that God was her means of survival.

. . .

Every word of God proves true; he is a shield to those who take refuge in him.

—Proverbs 30:5

Dear God, sometimes when the chips are really down, we feel as if you have forsaken us in the hour that we need you most. Our faith falters as we look for some confirmation of your plan for our lives. Then we are reminded that if we pick up the sword and the shield that you offer us, we will be able to properly defend ourselves. God, thank you for providing us with the tools we so desperately need to stand strong and tall in the face of adversity. Amen.

THIRTY-ONE

Déjà Vu

❦

PAT AND JACK WERE ON THEIR WAY to Whitewater to pick up their daughter Elizabeth from college. Pat could hardly contain her excitement. The whole family—Pat, Jack, Elizabeth, and Amanda—would be reunited for three glorious weeks during the Christmas holiday.

When they arrived at Elizabeth's dormitory, Pat walked briskly up to her room to help her with her bags. When she saw Liz at the end of the hall, she picked up her pace, anxious to get closer to her. She finally reached her side, pulling her into her arms, and giving her a big hug. "It's so good to see you again, mom," Elizabeth said. The hitch in Elizabeth's voice made Pat take a good hard look at her daughter. She looked so exhausted, with dark rings lining the bottom of her eyes. "Were your finals tough, honey?" her mother asked. "Yeah, mom. I'm really ready for a long, relaxing winter break at home." The three chatted amiably on the way home, talking excitedly about Christmas and all their plans.

Elizabeth's former boss had welcomed the notion of rehiring her during winter break. She had always been a conscientious worker, and, in his mind, you could never have too many of those. While Liz would have loved to sleep in late the next morning, she needed the money; so she got up early and headed off to work. It was great to see old friends and to fall into the rhythm of last summer's routine. But as the day progressed, she felt tired . . . so very tired. She found herself wishing that she had taken a few days off before heading back to work.

When Liz walked into the house that afternoon, Pat looked at her with alarm. She looked not only tired, but sick. As Pat held her hand to Elizabeth's forehead, she realized that she had a slight fever. "Liz, are you all right?" Pat asked with concern. "I feel miserable, mom. I have a sore throat, a fever, and a cough. I guess I burned the midnight oil too many nights preparing for those finals." With Christmas just two days away, Pat thought it made sense to have a doctor check her out. If they waited, it might be hard to find a doctor when they really needed one.

It was impossible to get Liz into their family doctor on such short notice; so Pat took her to a walk-in clinic. After doing a workup on Liz, the doctor there decided to send her downstairs for a chest x-ray. While Pat and Liz waited for the results, they talked about all sorts of things. But, somehow their conversation kept coming back to the situation at hand. Both hoped that Liz didn't have something serious such as bronchitis or pneumonia. After all, this was supposed to be her break from school, a time when she could relax and pick up the old threads with her family and friends. It would be unfortunate if illness kept her in bed for a good part of her time off.

Finally, the doctor came to see them, ushering them into his office. He told Pat and Liz he had found an unidentified mass on her chest x-ray. With no preamble, he said, "I think we're looking at lymphoma. I've called the oncology department, and they are expecting you immediately." Pat thought, "What? Isn't lymphoma cancer? How can they tell from an x-ray that Liz has cancer? Don't they need to do blood work or a biopsy or something?" But while Pat's mind was racing uncontrollably, she maintained a calm exterior. For Elizabeth's sake, she needed to remain in control.

As they headed up to oncology, Liz was bewildered. "Mom, isn't lymphoma cancer? Do I have *cancer*?" Pat reassured her daughter, telling her that the doctor was more than likely overreacting. She explained that she probably would have to go through more tests before they figured out what was wrong with her. "Liz, let's just take a deep breath and let the oncologist figure out what's going on, okay?"

Pat and Liz were immediately taken into Dr. Blankenship's office. She carefully reviewed the chest x-ray and told Elizabeth that she would like to order some blood work. When asked about the prospect of lymphoma, Dr. Blankenship looked up in surprise. "Liz, did you have some other tests? All I show is that you had a chest x-ray." "No," Liz said. "Well, then, it's definitely premature to be talking about your diagnosis at this point in time." Pat sighed with relief. At least *this* doctor was going through all the proper steps rather than jumping to premature conclusions.

Liz's blood work showed that her white blood cell count was, in fact, elevated. She definitely had some kind of infection or illness raging through her body. Dr. Blankenship next tested Liz for mononucleosis; the test results were positive. Liz had mono. Liz was told to get plenty of rest and to let her body's natural immune system do the rest. And that's what she did. By the time she headed back to college that January, she was feeling reasonably good, to the relief of her entire family. Cancer—what an unnecessary scare that was!

When Liz returned home from college that summer, Pat thought she still looked a bit tired. While she realized that college could be draining, she was concerned that traces of the mono might still be present in her system. So, she scheduled an appointment with their family doctor. When they arrived at Dr. Bruck's office, they chronicled the turn of events that had transpired the previous December. Dr. Bruck was quite surprised. No one had sent any of the test results to him. He questioned Pat, "Why did they do a chest x-ray? They never do one of those when they suspect mono." To Liz, he said, "Let's get another chest x-ray, Liz. I'd like to check and see if there's any sign of a mass in your chest now. In the meantime, I'll try to track down the first x-ray so we can compare the results."

Later that day, Pat received a phone call. Alarmingly, the mass was still in Liz's chest; in fact, it appeared to have grown in the past six months. Dr. Bruck was concerned and wanted to schedule Liz for an immediate biopsy. He explained that they needed to find out what was causing this growth because it clearly should not be there.

On the day of Liz's biopsy, Pat, Jack, and Amanda waited anxiously at the hospital. As Dr. Bruck approached them, he had a smile on his face. "Good news. The initial staining that the pathologist did tested negative for cancer. We'll have to culture the cells for the next few days, just to be sure, but we're pretty sure Liz doesn't have cancer." Hugs and kisses went around the circle, as Liz's family breathed an immense sigh of relief. While they still didn't know what was going on in Liz's body, the family felt *anything* would be better than having cancer at the age of twenty. For the second time, Pat felt like their family had managed to dodge the cancer bullet.

Two days later, Dr. Bruck called. He told Pat that the long-term pathology reports revealed that Liz had Hodgkin's lymphoma. Pat was stunned.

Her thoughts strayed . . . "Yes. No. Yes. No. Which is it? Does Liz have cancer or *not?*" She shook her head and redirected her thoughts, trying to focus on what the doctor was saying. She asked, "What about what you said two days ago? You said she didn't have cancer then." The doctor hesitated and then said, "Some people hear what they *want* to hear." Pat was stunned for the second time. What was he talking about? The whole family had clearly heard him say that the initial pathology had tested negative for cancer. Well, one thing was for sure; they were going to get a second opinion.

Concerned with the conflicting results, Liz and her family searched for a new oncologist that would give them the straight story. But Liz's new oncologist, Dr. Gabrus, confirmed everything that Dr. Bruck had previously said. Liz had cancer. While the news remained negative, Dr. Gabrus was so very kind, patiently answering any and all questions they had. Finally, Pat felt that someone was listening to her.

This felt like such a déjà vu moment for Pat and her husband, Jack. Twenty years earlier, when Pat was pregnant with Liz, they had received a phone call from Jack's brother, Mike. He had called to tell them that he had just been diagnosed with Hodgkin's lymphoma. Pat found herself wondering how two people in the same family could be diagnosed with the same exact cancer at the same juncture in their lives. It was a heck of a coincidence.

As Liz and her family went through the necessary motions of being educated on the appropriate next steps, the family learned that the standard protocol for Hodgkin's was a splenectomy followed by radiation. Liz handled every aspect of her surgery and treatment like a trouper. She continued to work through all of her treatments, never missing one day of work. She always exhibited a positive, fighting spirit, never once giving up. After going into complete remission, Liz headed back to UW-Whitewater to earn her college degree. All was well with Pat and her family once again.

As a direct result of being so closely touched by cancer, Liz's sister, Amanda, found herself strangely intrigued about pursuing a career in medicine. Four years younger than Liz, she had started moving in the direction of becoming a radiographer. After graduating from high school, she began training at one of the local hospitals to do just that. Amanda loved the career she had chosen.

One day on her way to work, Amanda found herself absently scratching her neck, when she felt a lump. She didn't think much of it at the time; but as the days passed, the lump didn't go away. Finally, she showed it to her mother. After all the difficult times Pat and her family had been through four years earlier with Liz, they certainly weren't going to take any chances. She called Dr. Bruck and asked to see him immediately.

Pat and Amanda were fortunate enough to get in to see their doctor the very next day. Dr. Bruck was careful to not overreact, suggesting that they "keep an eye on it" for a while. But, a few months later when Amanda developed an upper respiratory infection, he noticed that the hard, immovable knot was still there. He then opted to send Amanda to an Ear, Nose, and Throat (ENT) specialist. As the ENT felt the lump, he told Amanda and her mother, "This is definitely not normal. I'm not sure what it is, but I'm going to have it removed." The lump was removed, leaving a small scar as proof of its earlier existence. The phone call that Pat received, just a few short days later, resurfaced an even older scar. Amanda had Hodgkin's lymphoma.

Pat thought, "This is totally unbelievable. There has to be some mistake. There is no possible way that both of my daughters and my brother-in-law could all have had the same cancer at the same age." The whole situation was totally preposterous.

As her family came to grips with Amanda's diagnosis, Liz reassured them. "I've been through this before, mom. We can handle this. We know what to expect." But that wasn't to be the case. The protocol for Hodgkin's had dramatically changed since Liz's earlier diagnosis and treatment. Doctors had since found that they could diminish the intensity of the radiation by using a bimodal treatment: less radiation coupled with a few months of chemotherapy. Early signs were showing that this protocol significantly decreased the risk of latent breast cancer and other potential future complications. "Great," thought Pat. "Now I not only have to worry about dealing with Amanda's treatments, but I also have to worry about whether Liz's treatments were too harsh for her body."

Pat was overwhelmed. She cried; actually, she wailed with grief. While she had pulled herself through Liz's crisis, she no longer believed she had the strength and energy to make it through Amanda's diagnosis and treatments. She was grief-stricken. She was angry. She was worried. She found it difficult to sort through all of her emotions. Her husband, Jack, was a constant source of strength for Pat. He was so positive, constantly reassuring her that they would get through this. Pat's friends rallied at her side, helping the family out whenever or wherever they could. But it wasn't enough. Pat still felt lost and alone. Ultimately, she realized that she needed God's help. She prayed, elevating her concerns and worries up to God. He was the source of all goodness. He had healed Mike and Liz—He had the capacity to heal Amanda too.

Amanda's treatment protocol was far more demanding than Liz's had been. As Pat looked at her daughter, there were countless times during that year when she thought she would gladly have taken the cancer from Amanda's body and placed it into her own. It was so difficult for a mother to watch from the sidelines, as first one then the other daughter had to deal with cancer.

Amanda forged a very close and intimate relationship with Liz that year. She and her sister became soul mates, for no one truly understands what a cancer patient is going through like someone who has been there before. Liz recognized when Amanda needed an empathetic ear, an embracing hug, or a gentle shove. Their shared experience with Hodgkin's lymphoma at the age of twenty, bonded them together unlike anything else they had ever experienced.

Recently, Liz celebrated a very special day in her life. She got married. Standing by her side, as her maid of honor, her friend, her soul mate was her sister, Amanda.

. . .

For it is a credit to you if, being aware of God, you endure pain while suffering unjustly. If you endure when you are beaten for doing wrong, what credit is that? But if you endure when you do right and suffer for it, you have God's approval. For to this you have been called, because Christ also suffered for you, leaving you an example, so that you should follow in his steps.

—1 Peter 2:19–21

Lord, we have been told that there is no such thing as a coincidence— that all coincidences are merely divine inspiration. How can we reconcile, then, when coincidences happen that are so negative and debilitating? We understand that you do not inflict evil upon us and that the forces of good and evil are at work in our everyday world. But still we struggle to accept what is happening in our lives. Please show us the way. Amen.

THIRTY-TWO

The Power of Love

V IVIAN HAD STRUGGLED THROUGH a less than pleasant childhood. She had grown up in a home void of love and had been abused to the point where she questioned whether she would ever know the meaning of love. Then she met Bert, and her life began anew. Bert loved Vivian with his whole heart and soul. He adored her vibrant red hair. He rejoiced in the way a sunny smile slowly crept onto her face when he said something cute or sweet. He loved her exactly as she was, complete with all her faults. He asked nothing of her but that she return his love.

Vivian and Bert were tickled when their life was blessed with children. Vivian was determined to be the loving mother she had never had. And she made good on her promise–first when Claudia was born, then when Paul came into the world, and finally, when Linda graced their lives. She chose to stay at home rather than work, weaving herself into every aspect of her children's lives. She did anything and everything for them–they were her life.

When Linda was just a few months old, the unthinkable happened. Vivian was diagnosed with thyroid cancer. Doctors operated on her, hoping to remove the tumor, but the surgery was not as successful as they had expected. While they were able to remove a large portion of the tumor, it was impossible to eliminate it all. Vivian had cancer at a time in medical history when radiation and chemotherapy were deemed to be ineffective for her type of cancer, so there were no other options available to them. Doctors estimated that Vivian had six months to live. Her life now rested in God's hands.

Vivian's scar was menacing, reaching from just under her chin to the middle of her neck. Her shoulder was sunken to the point where she could neatly fit a golf ball in the hole. But none of that mattered to Vivian.

The scars and physical changes were all superficial. She had something that was so much more important *inside* of her. She had love . . . lots of it. In her mind, she had only just begun to live. She rationalized that each year she could remain alive would be one more precious year with Bert and her children. Her will to live was unquenchable.

Vivian continued to go in for checkups on a regular basis, but diagnostic equipment was not what it is today. So there was no easy way to determine if the growth of the cancer had been retarded or if it was continuing to grow. Eventually, with Vivian still alive and doing well, the doctor chose to perform a second surgery on her. He successfully removed more of Vivian's tumor, but once again left traces of cancer intact in her body. There was no safe way to remove it. On the positive side, the tumor had not grown, and the doctor was encouraged by Vivian's good health. He urged her to keep doing whatever she was doing because it appeared to be working. So Vivian and Bert did just that.

A short time later, Vivian was floored when she discovered she was pregnant with her fourth child. While her doctor had encouraged her to live her life, pregnancy was not on his list of suggested activities. As this new life began to grow inside of Vivian, it reinvigorated her will to live. She was a mother and a good one at that. She intended on living for a long, long time to administer to the needs of all of her children. But first she had to get through the pregnancy.

Amazingly, the pregnancy proceeded without a hitch. Nine months later, a perfectly healthy little baby girl, Stephanie, was born. Vivian and Bert were elated. Life with her husband and children continued to move forward, with Vivian relishing each moment. She volunteered as a Brownie leader, a Girl Scout leader, and as a worker in the school cafeteria, all with the goal of being as close to her children as possible. She cherished each moment with her family, never knowing when it would be her last.

The years flew by. In the eight years since Vivian's initial diagnosis, the diagnostic equipment had improved to the point where doctors could finally get a definitive read on the status of Vivian's untreated thyroid cancer. To the shock of all, there was absolutely no trace of cancer in Vivian's body. The doctors assured her that medicine could not take the credit for her cure, but that God's hand was at work in her life. Vivian had so believed in the power of love that she had been unwilling to accept any other prognosis. With God's love, she was cancer-free.

. . .

If I speak in the tongues of mortals and of angels, but do not have love, I am a noisy gong or a clanging cymbal. And if I have prophetic powers, and understand all mysteries and all knowledge, and if I have all faith, so as to remove mountains, but do not have love, I am nothing. If I give away all my possessions, and if I hand over my body so that I may boast, but do not have love, I gain nothing.

—1 Corinthians 13:1–3

Dear God, who are we to question the miracles that you perform? Many see your wondrous deeds and question whether it really happened or not. For those who believe in your goodness, they are rewarded with the gift of your miracles day after day. Please open our eyes so that we may see the bounty of all you do for us. Amen.

THIRTY-THREE

Laughter Is the Best Medicine

❧

STEVE WAS A FIREFIGHTER like his father before him. He hadn't intended to be. He had gone off to college, intending to pursue an entirely different career. But somehow, his love for the fire department had been like a magnet, drawing him back to his ultimate destiny.

Steve loved his life as a firefighter. Each day he had the ability to positively impact the lives of others. He liked to help people and especially enjoyed making them laugh. His use of humor was renowned around the fire station, almost revered. He was the one who always pulled pranks and practical jokes at the station, often when the other firefighters least expected it.

Steve was forty-seven when he was diagnosed with testicular cancer. That, by itself, was a joke of sorts. Testicular cancer was known as a "young man's" disease, usually inflicting men in their twenties. He was told that first on the docket was surgery. If successful and there was no lymph node involvement, he could get on with his life shortly thereafter. He was told not to worry–it was a fairly routine surgery. So Steve approached the surgery with little concern. The surgeon removed the tumor, took out a few lymph nodes, and closed Steve back up again. When he awoke from surgery, the doctor informed him that the cancer had been self-contained and he was cancer-free.

A few days later, the biopsy results returned. Steve's doctor was totally taken aback by the pathologist's findings. The lymph nodes had tested positive for cancer. What was even more shocking was that it was not testicular cancer, but a second, unrelated type of cancer. To insure that neither cancer returned, Steve would have to undergo chemotherapy. The first week of chemo would be administered in the hospital each day, Monday through Friday. The following two weeks would involve one outpatient infusion per week. Then the cycle would repeat itself twice. Steve began his treatments immediately.

The chemotherapy made Steve ill. Shakes and shivers racked his body as he donned layer after layer of clothing. Pain settled in his lower back, making him extremely uncomfortable. Steve's demeanor was serious and dour. He found it extremely difficult to get himself up and moving each day. The sense of humor that had once been his constant companion was lost.

Then one day, Steve's hair began to fall out, causing his funny bone to kick in. He handed a vacuum cleaner to his sons–Nick (twelve) and Sam (ten)–and asked them to write their names on his head. He promised them he would go to the fire station the very next day and show their handiwork off to the other firefighters. At first, the boys were a little timid and, quite honestly, a bit frightened. After all, what dad would ever give his sons *permission* to vacuum their names on the top of his head? But eventually, Steve prodded them into creating a masterpiece. In the end, Nick actually became enthused about the art project he had created. Being a big fan of Austin Powers, he told his dad he wanted to shave his own head and be "Mini Me." Since Steve didn't think his wife would approve, he chose to buy Nick a bald skullcap instead. Nick put his cap on and looked just like his dad, without having to touch a hair on his head.

Steve made a point of visiting his buddies at the station the next day, complete with his patchwork quilt head. The guys were so impressed with Steve's sense of humor that they decided to return the favor. The next time he was hospitalized for chemotherapy, twelve fellow firefighters walked into Steve's room with shaved heads. They had made a pact–none of them had told their wives what they were doing. Not only had they surprised Steve, but they had also totally shocked their wives in the process!

While the other firefighters saw Steve laughing and clowning around, truth be known, he was floundering inside. Steve had only turned to laughter because it was his natural defense mechanism during times of stress. It was his way of coping with the impossible. But ever so slowly, Steve found himself turning to laughter more and more often. He started by pulling practical jokes on the nurses at the hospital. In the beginning, he wasn't trying to make their lives more enjoyable; instead, he was trying to put himself in better spirits. Ironically, however, Steve found that the more he joked, the more he teased out smiles and giggles from nurses and cancer patients alike. One cancer patient who had never once smiled during treatment was suddenly smirking along with everyone else. The more those around him found humor in his pranks, the more Steve wanted to make just one more patient a little happier during the cancer journey.

It all began, innocently enough, with Steve's bald head. In a comical sort of way, Steve had started to affectionately call himself "bald eagle." One day, when his IV machine let out its loud, shrill beep, demanding the attention of a nurse, Steve squawked like a baby eagle. He chidingly declared across the room to the nurses, "You feed me. I get strong. I fly away." That day became the rallying cry for the staff and patients to begin their own pranks. Steve thought, "Let the games begin!"

For Steve's next chemotherapy treatment, he came to the hospital with a Mohawk glued to the top of his head. He had also glued a droopy moustache to his face and fuzzy hair to his chest. As he entered the hospital, he felt eight feet tall, with his Mohawk reaching high toward the ceiling. Heads turned left and right as he passed visitors, patients, and staff. The looks on people's faces ranged from shock to disapproval to bewilderment to humor. Of course, no one understood the real story behind Steve's antics until he entered the chemo room. He confidently strode into the room and announced to the group, "Don't worry, I'm just having a bad hair day." The laughter began rippling across the room until everyone was laughing uproariously. It was as if a dark cloud had lifted and a ray of sunshine had filtered through the darkness in the room.

It didn't take long for the staff and patients to participate in Steve's games. It seemed that everyone was just looking for an excuse to act silly and outrageous during an extremely difficult time in his or her life. On Steve's next day of treatment, two patients showed up with shaved heads, except for one small line of hair running through the middle of their heads. Steve's nurses, Sue and Carol, also found it was fun to get into the act. They decided if Steve was going to cry like a baby eagle, then they would provide him with the right "digs" to help with his role-playing efforts. When he arrived for his next chemotherapy treatment, he took one look at the chair he usually occupied and found the laughter uncontrollably bubbling out of him. The nurses had made an eagle's nest for Steve. There were sticks and branches sticking out of his IV pumps and a special nest for Steve to sit in. Soon there was a chorus of birdcalls throughout the chemo room. One patient had perfected the call of a pigeon, another a condor. All the birds chirped in unison, leaving the nurses rolling in laughter and innocent bystanders wondering what the heck could possibly be so funny about cancer patients being infused with drugs. The practical jokes continued throughout treatment. Steve added to the frivolities by buying eagle beaks for the nurses. On one particular day, the staff wove gummy worms into the nostrils of their beaks and attempted to feed the baby eagle, Steve, while he roosted in his nest.

That was when Steve realized that God had reached down and pressed him into action. God intended for Steve to use his sense of humor and his unerring ability to bring sunshine to the lives of fellow cancer patients. During Steve's chemotherapy treatments, each patient and nurse in that room learned the art of leaning on one another for support, finding that laughter is indeed the best medicine.

. . .

A cheerful heart is a good medicine

—Proverbs 17:22a

Dear God, we understand that the attitude we display can have a profound effect on how we make our journey through life. But sometimes it's hard to find humor in the mundane, laughter in adversity, and joy during difficult times. Please help us spread our joy to those in need. Amen.

Other books from
The Pilgrim Press

Pilgrim Prayers for Single Fathers

DAVID ALBERT FARMER

Farmer, a divorced father, shares the trials, tribulations, and joys he has
experienced raising his two sons as a single father. Finances, homework,
divorce, sex, and dating are some of the many topics he discusses.
Farmer attracts his readers' attention by beginning each entry with a
letter addressing a specific issue. He continues with a Scripture passage,
prayer, and an interesting or informative passage. Useful Internet sites
are also shared with single dads.

ISBN 0-8298-1594-5/paper/128 pg/**$12.00**

Pilgrim Prayers for Mealtime

ALEXANDER CAMPBELL

This is the ideal resource for families, congregations, and organizations
that hold events in which meals are shared. It is a welcome escape from
a quick, repetitious, and shallow approach to praying as participants are
invited to put their whole hearts, minds, and souls into reading or
hearing the Scripture and praying to God. Each prayer relates to a
particular Scripture passage and corresponds to the themes of
thankfulness and praise.

ISBN 0-8298-1552-X/paper/128 pg/**$10.00**

Pilgrim Prayers for Leading Worship

JOHN E. BIEGERT

This resource focuses on prayers for use by worship leaders–clergy and
lay. It has been carefully designed to follow the liturgical year, yet also
includes invocations and prayers for other occasions.

ISBN 0-8298-1567-8/paper/128 pg/**$10.00**

Pilgrim Prayers for Single Mothers

MICHELE HOWE

This resource is one of the few books to address a single mother's faith or spirituality. The wide-ranging experiences of single mothers are briefly described in narrative form, followed by prayer based on an appropriate Scripture passage. Finances, friendship, fear, loneliness, anger, and encouragement are some of the topics embraced.

ISBN 0-8298-1472-8/paper/128 pg/**$10.00**

Pilgrim Prayers for Grandmothers Raising Grandchildren

LINDA H. HOLLIES

Best-selling author Linda Hollies, who with her husband is raising her grandson, has written an inspirational book for the ever-increasing number of grandmothers who are raising their grandchildren. The stories and prayers will provide encouragement and comfort for the journey.

ISBN 0-8298-1490-6/paper/128 pg/**$10.00**

Pilgrim Prayers for Church Choirs

KENNETH JOHNSON

Before worship, pastors usually gather with the choir for prayer. This unique resource provides short prayers for use by pastors, music directors, and those who are involved with music ministry. It is based on the Revised Common Lectionary and follows the liturgical year.

ISBN 0-8298-1505-8/paper/128 pg/**$10.00**

To order these or any other books from The Pilgrim Press call or write to:

The Pilgrim Press
700 Prospect Avenue East
Cleveland, Ohio 44115-1100

Phone orders: 1.800-537.3394 • Fax orders: 216.736.2206

Please include shipping charges of $4.00 for the first book and $0.75 for each additional book.

Or order from our Web sites at www.pilgrimpress.com and www.ucpress.com.

Prices subject to change without notice.